LEGENDS DIE YOUNG

BRIAN BARCELONA

LEGENDS DIE YOUNG

CHARISMA
HOUSE

Legends Die Young by Brian Barcelona
Published by Charisma House, an imprint of Charisma Media
1150 Greenwood Blvd., Lake Mary, Florida 32746

Copyright © 2024 by Brian Barcelona. All rights reserved.

Unless otherwise noted, all Scripture quotations are taken from the (NASB®) New American Standard Bible®, Copyright © 1960, 1971, 1977, 1995 by The Lockman Foundation. Used by permission. All rights reserved. www.lockman.org

Scripture quotations marked esv are from The ESV® Bible (The Holy Bible, English Standard Version®), copyright © 2001 by Crossway, a publishing ministry of Good News Publishers. Used by permission. All rights reserved.

Scripture quotations marked kjv are from the King James Version of the Bible.

Scripture quotations marked nasb are taken from the (NASB®) New American Standard Bible®, Copyright © 1960, 1971, 1977, 1995, 2020 by The Lockman Foundation. Used by permission. All rights reserved. www.lockman.org

Scripture quotations marked niv are taken from the Holy Bible, New International Version®, NIV®. Copyright © 1973, 1978, 1984, 2011 by Biblica, Inc.® Used by permission of Zondervan. All rights reserved worldwide. www.zondervan.com. The "NIV" and "New International Version" are trademarks registered in the United States Patent and Trademark Office by Biblica, Inc.®

Scripture quotations marked nkjv are taken from the New King James Version®. Copyright © 1982 by Thomas Nelson. Used by permission. All rights reserved.

Cover design by Manny Gaitan

While the author has made every effort to provide accurate, up-to-date source information at the time of publication, statistics and other data are constantly updated. Neither the publisher nor the author assumes any responsibility for errors or for changes that occur after publication. Further, the publisher and author do not have any control over and do not assume any responsibility for third-party websites or their content.

For more resources like this, visit MyCharismaShop.com and the author's website at brianbarcelona.com.

Cataloging-in-Publication Data is on file with the Library of Congress.

International Standard Book Number: 978-1-63641-410-2
E-book ISBN: 978-1-63641-411-9

1 2024
Printed in the United States of America

Most Charisma Media products are available at special quantity discounts for bulk purchase for sales promotions, premiums, fund-raising, and educational needs. For details, call us at (407) 333-0600 or visit our website at www.charismamedia.com.

I want to dedicate this book to mothers and fathers who have stood in the faith without wavering for decades, to pastors who have lived out the gospel—although not being famous, they have been faithful. I want to dedicate this book to the persecuted church around the world, to whom Christianity has looked like hardship even unto death.

TABLE OF CONTENTS

Thanks xi
Introduction xiii

Chapter 1	Forsake	1
Chapter 2	Redeemed	22
Chapter 3	Offended	49
Chapter 4	Betrayal	77
Chapter 5	Bitterness	94
Chapter 6	Unforgiveness	112
Chapter 7	Suffering	137
Chapter 8	Disappointment	155
Chapter 9	Complaining	177
Chapter 10	How to Die	190

Notes 211

THANKS

Rob Parker, I would like to express my deepest gratitude for your invaluable contribution to this book. Your dedication, time, and unwavering commitment to pouring not just knowledge but also your heart into this project have made a profound impact.

I would also like to thank the following people for their contributions because without them this book would not be the same: Lou Engle, Michael Miller, Heidi Baker, Todd White, Brian "Head" Welch, Aaron Smith, Tim Bruce, Melissa Smith, Michael Koulianos, the anonymous mother, and the anonymous pastor.

Kala Boss, thank you for the countless hours of putting this book together.

INTRODUCTION

Jesus teaches that to find our lives, we must lose them. Life is found when we die. Think about this for a moment. Yet many of us fear death—not the physical kind but the death of our fleshly desires and ambitions. Despite Jesus' teachings, many believers today are still afraid to die to themselves, to pick up their crosses and deny themselves. This has become one of the most countercultural messages of our time. As Christians, the moment we accept Christ, we are crucified with Him (Gal. 2:20), meaning we no longer cling to our own rights. Every right we had was nailed to the cross—the right to be offended, bitter, angry, unforgiving, critical, and even right. These are contributing to what I believe is a great falling away from, or deconstruction of, the faith, prevalent in today's generation.

The world is filled with self-help books aimed at keeping you alive and helping you become the best version of yourself. Thousands of social media pages, even Christian ones, are dedicated to promoting self-achievement. However, the Bible presents a different narrative. Jesus lived and taught the opposite, urging His followers to emulate His example.

We never see a Jesus who was entitled or overly concerned with His own opinions or rights. He never played the victim of hurt and pain. Jesus didn't defend against wrongs done to Him or keep only those who would benefit Him close—consider His relationship with Judas.

So what is deconstruction? *Deconstruction* is just another term for falling away. Jesus never instructed us to become deconstructionists; He called us to be disciples. Discipleship is how Jesus taught His followers the ways of His Father by focusing less on personal opinions and more on understanding God's Word and His views.

If the trend of young people falling away and deconstructing were a sickness, then I believe the chapters in this book would serve as the medicine. It doesn't take rocket science or being a pastor to recognize that the hardships of life and of our faith, when not viewed through the lens of the Bible and the life Jesus called us to live, can become our greatest stumbling blocks. Even the disciples, who had grown strong in their faith over three years, experienced despair and hardship at the sight of Jesus going to the cross; it caused them to scatter and some to return to their former occupations. They even lost their faith within three days, evidenced by their initial disbelief in the women's report of His resurrection (Mark 16:10–11).

Whether your faith feels stronger than ever or you're struggling to maintain your relationship with God, this book is for you. It offers keys to unlocking the cages we find ourselves in. If you have walked away from your faith in Christ, this book is also for you. The stories you will read are not only from titled leaders but from people with genuine hearts, real emotions, real pain, and real experiences of dying to themselves to keep their faith alive.

There can be no coexistence of your life and your faith—one must die, and one must live. "To live is Christ and to die is gain" (Phil. 1:21). Few books other than the Bible aim to teach you how to die. Again, I am not referring to physical death; I am talking about dying to your old self and to whom God never intended you to be. In reality we choose to either die to ourselves or let our faith die. No martyrs ever went to their death who hadn't already died to themselves long before their physical deaths.

To quote a dear friend and pastor, "The fall away of youth today I believe can be credited to the watered-down gospel we have given and been given for years and not teaching them to die."[1]

LEGENDS DIE YOUNG

As we begin this journey, my hope is that you will journey through the Scriptures and engage in many conversations with the Holy Spirit about the topics discussed. I hope you wrestle with yourself over topics that are difficult to hear, and I have included "Make It Personal" questions at the end of each chapter to help you do that. Write your responses down and consider discussing them with a small group of trusted believers. Now more than ever, I hope a joyful desire to die to yourself and lay your life down arises within you. And I hope your priorities shift and you find your heart and will leaning more toward obeying God.

If you're wondering why the title of this book is *Legends Die Young*, I will tell you. I've so often heard the word *legend* thrown around after I would preach, or it's been used by someone expressing pride in me. This led me to deeply consider what truly makes a legend. Who are legends to me? Whether they are Black, White, Hispanic, involved in politics or ministry, or simply a mom or dad I know, one common thread unites them—they all laid down their lives.

So often we glamorize those we consider legends for their cars, homes, or wealth, or the impact they've made in the world. We highlight their successes, not realizing that these monumental moments were built on small, faithful acts, giving a little more each day.

As Christians we have the honor of following in the footsteps of the greatest legend—Jesus Christ. He walked the earth, died on the cross, and rose again. He was a legend who died young, at the age of thirty-three. But He was also a legend who died to Himself early in life. From the earliest accounts, when

Jesus was twelve and in the temple, to His last moments on the cross, we see a man continually devoted to His Father's business, whose greatest desire was to bring His Father joy.

May our lives mirror His. May our lives bring Him joy. May He find faith on earth when He returns, and may the Lamb receive the reward of His suffering. This book is a guide to laying down your life and following Jesus—our ultimate example, our ultimate legend.

Chapter 1

FORSAKE

WHEN I OBSERVE the current state of the church, I can understand the disappointment many are feeling today. From news articles to wars waged in social media comment sections among believers to the differing opinions, mistrust of leadership, and recurring issues across generations, I can see why this could be disheartening. Additionally, I see how for many, their experience of Jesus has become bitter—whether due to personal failings, mishandling of funds, or other distressing situations. In this chapter I won't delve into specific individuals, stories, or headline news, nor will I engage in debates about how things might have been better handled. Instead, I simply want to start off by acknowledging that I can see why people have felt validated in both leaving the church and ultimately walking away from their faith in Jesus Christ.

Many people find themselves caught between what they do not wish to see and what they deeply long for. In this valley of decision, numerous individuals are losing their faith, turning their backs on the cross, and choosing not to follow Christ. I am not referring to those who were on the fence or who never fully committed to following Jesus. Instead, I recognize those who were once strong believers, who served faithfully and even felt called to ministry. I have also seen people creating their own version of the Jesus they want to follow, along with their personalized gospels that cater to their needs, wants, hurts, and pains. But at the same time, they fail to realize that this self-fashioned belief in a God made in their own image will not withstand the test of time.

Before we delve deeper, let me define *deconstruction*.

Although there are many aspects of deconstruction, I will focus on just a few in this chapter. Deconstruction is not a new concept; it was first introduced in the 1960s by a French philosopher named Jacques Derrida. According to one source, "*Deconstruction* doesn't actually mean 'demolition;' instead it means 'breaking down' or analyzing something (especially the words in a work of fiction or nonfiction) to discover its true significance, which is supposedly almost never exactly what the author intended."[1]

Another perspective on deconstruction suggests: "The most extreme form of deconstruction, which denies core doctrines of Christian orthodoxy, [equates to] deconversion or apostasy. It might be better described as destruction or demolition of the faith, seeking to 'burn it all down' or twist it into an unrecognizable shape."[2] This statement might seem bold, as many would argue that deconstructing is not about losing their faith but rather discarding aspects that were never meant to be part of the faith.

We've seen this phenomenon more than ever recently. When we struggle to come to grips with our experiences or face the reality that God allows us to endure trials (but never abandons us in the process), we often choose to form a version of God that we prefer to follow. A prime example of this is the people of Israel during the time of Moses. Despite being delivered out of Egypt, they grew offended, impatient, and uncertain of God's larger plan. This dissatisfaction led them to create idols with their own hands to worship. (See Exodus 32–34.) Similarly, many of us do the same today.

Turning Their Backs on Christ

I believe a significant focus of Jesus' ministry was on discipleship because the very issues we encounter today were also prevalent two thousand years ago. They too contended with false prophets, leaders who did not preach the full truth, rigorous political cultures, persecution within and outside the church, sexual immorality, and witchcraft and divination. As the scripture says, "There is nothing new under the sun" (Eccles. 1:9).

Church tradition tells us that all disciples except John the Beloved died horrendous deaths. Their ability to lay down their lives stemmed from having "died" long before their actual deaths. They spent three years journeying with Jesus, learning the essence of discipleship—where discipleship thrives, deconstruction does not. They also learned to lay down their lives daily, not just in a one-time altar call at a local church. You see, dying daily is a practice you live out each day, and the only way to become good at dying daily is to continue this practice daily.

I wholeheartedly believe that those I know who have left the faith, and perhaps those you know too, were just a few conversations away from salvaging their shipwrecked faith. Those who walked away bitter, feeling justified or being justified in their hurt, might have had a different outcome had they understood the broader narrative of God. I believe the chapters ahead will paint this picture and illustrate the hardships and pains associated with a life devoted to Christ.

We must acknowledge that just as God has a narrative and agenda for your life, so does the devil. The devil is cunning and deceitful and has studied humanity for thousands of years. His tactics remain the same as they were in the beginning of time, always questioning, "Did God really say…?" (Gen. 3:1, NIV). Do you not think he knows how to lead people astray? He even believed he could lead Jesus astray in the desert of temptation.

While I don't want to merely spiritualize the real pain we experience, I must acknowledge the existence of a spiritual realm. There is a battle for our souls between light and darkness. Doubts, if unaddressed, can lead us to turn away from Christ. Although I believe nothing can pluck us from God's hand, we do have the free will to walk away if we so choose.

Many from my teenage years who got saved with me sadly no longer follow Jesus. Our enduring trials, hardships, and disagreements were probably similar. What distinguishes those who have remained faithful from those who have fallen away is likely simpler than we think. Following I list three safeguards that can help you continue following Jesus until the end of your days, and that offer hope that the solution to your crisis is not deconstruction but discipleship.

Safeguard 1: The Word

There is a hill that I will die on, which I will mention as the first step to not turning our backs on Christ—it's that the Word of God is the ultimate authority. The Word of God supersedes my opinion, my experiences, and even my emotions and thoughts about various situations because the Word is Jesus (John 1). The Word of God is the boundary line that keeps me from entering dangerous areas where I am susceptible to the devil's attacks on my mind and heart. The Word is a guiding light, a lamp unto my feet, preventing me from falling into holes I cannot escape (Ps. 119:105). The Word of God is a sword, enabling me to fight when my faith is under attack.

A key factor I have seen among those who leave the faith is that one of the first things they stop doing is reading the Word. Posts on social media or music become their truth. Conversations with friends become their truth. And the Word of God takes a back seat as they let others take the wheel of their faith, driving them to places they never imagined they would go. No, when I talk about reading the Word, I am not referring to just religiously reading the Bible to say you did it. I am talking about consuming the Word and letting it wash your soul. I am talking about allowing the very words of Jesus to be seen not as a historical text but as a direct letter to you.

Time and again I have seen that when the Bible becomes a

decoration on your table, your faith becomes the same. The Bible is God's conversation with you; it's a way He speaks, a way He guides. In the greatest temptation Jesus ever faced, He knew that the only thing that would withstand His testing was the Word.

But don't forget that Satan also knows the Word. He knows it because he is bound to it. It is also his boundary line that he cannot cross. The Bible says no temptation has seized you except what is common to man, and God is just and will always provide a way out (1 Cor. 10:13). I believe the way out is the Word. As Satan twisted the Bible to tempt Jesus to step outside God's boundary, Jesus knew the Word. In Jesus' vulnerable state, where not even a piece of bread had touched His lips in forty days, the Word was what filled His belly.

Don't let the Word become something that is easily forfeited on the altar of offense, anger, or hypocrisy. It's easy to blame the Word when we see someone who claims to know the Word mistreat us in a way that the Word would never condone. But you have to know something about the Bible—it stands true and alone as a book with one author and millions of readers. Just because someone reads it doesn't mean that the book has read them. There are also situations where you might know churches or individuals that have used the Word to justify a wrong action. Again, I will say this: Reading the Word should ultimately lead you to knowing the author. Those who read the Word and misuse it are not those who have gotten to know the author.

Since the day I met Rob Parker, his life has been nothing but a blessing. From his wisdom, his patience, and his love, he has truly been a father to me and One Voice Student Missions. He has also served on the board of One Voice for many years, seeing our ministry grow from its infancy to where it is today. I asked him to share his insights on the importance of engaging with God's Word.

Rob Parker

The Bible is made up of sixty-six books and letters written by more than forty authors over a period of approximately fifteen hundred years. The Bible was written in three languages—Hebrew; Koine, or common Greek; and Aramaic—on three continents: Asia, Africa, and Europe. The Bible contains a divine message, also known as "the Word of God," and it is one continuous and consistent storyline that begins in Genesis and ends in Revelation. With all these contributing authors over such a period of time on different continents, its message remains the same and does not contradict itself. It is impossible for man to create such a document. The Bible is the Word of God; you can count on it.

> For the word of God is alive and active. Sharper than any double-edged sword, it penetrates even to dividing soul and spirit, joints and marrow; it judges the thoughts and attitudes of the heart.
> —Hebrews 4:12, niv

The Bible is alive; it is a living, breathing document. There is no other book like it that has the ability to speak to us on such a personal level. It is precise and so sharp that it can separate between our soul and our spirit. The Word of God will actually reveal to us our thoughts and our motives and all that is unhealthy and ungodly. Additionally, it will show us how to live.

> All Scripture is God-breathed and is useful for teaching, rebuking, correcting and training in righteousness, so that the servant of God may be thoroughly equipped for every good work.
> —2 Timothy 3:16–17, niv

All Scripture is spoken, breathed by God. Every

word in the Bible is from Yahweh, and it's true in every situation with every person on every continent and every time period of history. It is not dated and never fails to be relevant because it was written for your soul. The Word teaches us how to live, walk, and serve. The Word is our helper, teacher, and guide. It will help you walk in righteousness.

> Do not merely listen to the word, and so deceive yourselves. Do what it says.
> —JAMES 1:22, NIV

We cannot be listeners of the Word only, but we have to be doers. We have to read it, know what it says, bow our hearts to it, repent of arguing with it, and cry out to God for the grace to understand it and do it. It's not impossible; it only takes time. God has given you His Word because He wants His best for you and wants you to walk in freedom and life.

> How can a young man keep his way pure? By guarding it according to your word.
> —PSALM 119:9, ESV

The only hope that you and I have is the Word of God. We must read it, digest it, meditate upon it, and fix our minds on it. Our only hope for purity of thought and behavior is that we know the Word; we must let it wash us and cleanse us from wrong thoughts and unhealthy emotions. Ask the Lord for the spirit of revelation and understanding. Then ask Him for grace—that is, the divine empowerment to obey His word.

> Heaven and earth will pass away, but my words will never pass away.
> —MATTHEW 24:35, NIV

The Word of God will remain forever. It is trustworthy, consistent, and dependable. You never have to doubt God's Word. You can lean your heart in to it. Embrace it—it will never lead you astray.

> Jesus answered, "It is written: 'Man shall not live on bread alone, but on every word that comes from the mouth of God.'"
> —MATTHEW 4:4, NIV

Jesus, who is the Word of God in the flesh, uses the Word of God to make His point about the importance of feasting on the Word of God. We cannot truly survive just on natural food; we must eat, devour, the Word of God. His words are what sustain us and give us nutrients and all needed for living. His Word really is our bread, where we find our strength.

> Therefore, get rid of all moral filth and the evil that is so prevalent and humbly accept the word planted in you, which can save you.
> —JAMES 1:21, NIV

This very Bible verse makes it clear that the Scriptures are never irrelevant. This Bible verse clearly communicates the situation that we are currently living in. The instruction God is trying to give us is accept the Word of God, don't fight it, don't challenge it, and don't put it on trial. Receive it, accept it, ingest it, feed upon it, and devour it so that it can save you. God loves us, and therefore He has given us His Word. It is the kindest, most thoughtful thing He can do for us. It is our path to life, mental health, fulfillment, and identity.

> I have hidden your word in my heart that I might not sin against you.
> —PSALM 119:11, NIV

Behavior modification and trying to conquer the sin in our lives that we're all too familiar with are futile exercises. We have no hope of any kind of victory over sin apart from the grace of God operating in our members and knowing and hiding the Word of God within us. When we know His Word, take it unto ourselves, and hide it in our hearts, this is the only protection against a sinful life. When we know His Word, then we know His voice. When we know His voice, we can separate it from all the other voices that are clamoring in our heads. When we know His voice, then we can follow Him.

When we do not read the Word of God, we will not be able to get our minds renewed, discern the will of God, or do the will of God (Rom. 12:2). When we read His Word and put ourselves before it, think about it, and meditate upon it, it has a washing and cleansing effect. When we regularly read the Word of God, it washes the world off of us (Eph. 5:25–26). The Word of God creates safe boundaries for us; it leads us on the path and the way that we should walk. The Word of God is our refuge; it's our strength; it's the place that we find safety in peace. The Word is our safe place.

I encourage you to engage with the Word of God, reading it and letting it wash your soul and renew your mind. When we have a lifestyle of again engaging with God's Word, we will develop a renewed mind, thinking more clearly. When Bible reading and meditation become part of our lives, then He can fill us with the peace of God that surpasses understanding. This means there is a peace available to you and me that surpasses understanding. His Word can deliver us from anxiety, depression, and every unhealthy, negative thought or emotion and can teach us to walk in joy-filled righteousness. I encourage you today—feast on His Word.

Safeguard 2: Prayer

Our direct communication with God—our prayer life—is the binding glue in our relationship with Him. Prayer was never meant to be an emergency line we call occasionally or a ritual performed on the way to church; it is a personal, private dialogue where we bare our souls to God, sharing our issues, hurts, sins, and anguishes. Prayer was always intended to be the first place we process our issues, even before we turn to anyone else, because many of our concerns would likely never reach another person if we brought them to God in prayer first.

Prayer is often the second priority to falter in a believer's life after the Word. In fact it has been said that sin diminishes your desire for prayer while prayer diminishes your desire for sin. Yet prayer is frequently undervalued or mocked, especially in difficult situations. Common doubts such as "Why pray? Will God really help me?" reflect a misunderstanding of prayer's purpose. It's not meant to be a laundry list of chores for God or a one-sided conversation but a dynamic two-way interaction where God also speaks to us.

The tearing of the temple veil at Jesus' death symbolized the end of distant, mediated communication with God. He destroyed that barrier to establish a direct, anytime line of communication with us, facilitated by the sacrifice of His Son. God desired a direct line of communication so that at any moment, because of the price His Son paid, you could converse with the Creator of the world.

A significant misconception is that if God doesn't respond immediately or audibly, He isn't listening. Yet silence doesn't signify absence. In prayer God often allows us to decide based on our understanding of His will, without requiring constant reaffirmation.

I have often observed in Spirit-filled communities that people compare how they hear God; some consistently hear

Him through dreams, visions, prophetic words, or the Word, or in their hearts. Others feel that their prayer life and communication with God must be nonexistent because it doesn't resemble that of others. This comparison has long been a trap used by the devil to make people believe that if their relationship with God and prayer life don't look like someone else's, they must not be real. However, that couldn't be further from the truth.

I have four children—Zoe, Everlyse, Jedidiah, and Eden—who are all very different. Each of us has a unique relationship, though they all carry my blood in their veins. They also communicate with me differently. While my son freely expresses his thoughts and feelings, my daughter Everlyse is more reserved. Zoe might hesitate to share the truth at times, whereas Everlyse does not. I could not say that any one of my children has a better line of communication with me. Rather, each has a unique way of communicating with me, and it is this uniqueness that makes our relationships special.

You might feel discouraged reading this, or you may be thinking of someone in a place—or even find yourself in a place—where prayer has dissipated or is completely nonexistent because of moments when they (or you) felt God was silent. But take heart; just as Jesus was in the garden and spoke to His Father, saying, "Not my will, but yours" (Luke 22:42, NIV), the Scriptures do not indicate that God spoke back. This suggests that Jesus either knew in His heart what He was to do or that the Father chose to remain silent.

I can't tell you how many times my children have approached me late at night with a plea: "Dad, can I eat this candy even though it's late and I need to go to bed?" Often I don't respond; I just give them "the look." They laugh and return the candy to the pantry, understanding our household rules and my expectations. Similarly, when God has remained silent in my life, I have found beauty in those moments. His silence allows me to make decisions based on my understanding of His nature and His will, without needing further confirmation of what He has already asked of me.

Prayer is the anchor that can sustain you when your faith feels as if it is unraveling. When all other dialogues falter, your conversation with God remains steadfast. Notably, when the disciples had the opportunity to ask Jesus to teach them anything in Luke 11, they chose to learn how to pray. I don't know if they asked this aware that their Savior and friend would not be with them forever, but I believe the wisdom in that question is what sustained them through many situations.

SAFEGUARD 3: FRIENDS

This third safeguard is crucial in keeping you following Jesus until the end: the influence of friends. "Friends" often become pivotal, either sustaining someone's commitment to Jesus or contributing to their falling away during crises of faith, periods of doubt, or deconstruction. As the Bible warns, "Bad company corrupts good character" (1 Cor. 15:33, NIV). I stand here today not solely because I consistently read my Bible or just dug myself in prayer when necessary.

I am here today because during tough times, godly people surrounded me and spoke truth into my life. I'm not saying it was always easy to hear, but they reminded me of who I am in God. They reminded me of His promises when I only saw disappointment, and of the grace and mercy I had received when I was angry or felt offended. When I was ready to give up, they sat with me, prayed, and shared the Word. Your friends will either make or break your faith. Those whom you allow into the sacred places of your heart will either lead you to Christ or, like Job's friends, try to lead you away from God. (See Job 4–25.)

The Bible doesn't detail off-record conversations or moments of fear and doubt among the disciples, but living in community for over a decade has taught me that such moments inevitably arise. We need to encourage each other, stand together, speak truths in love, and forgive. Looking at Job's life, we see how friends can significantly influence us—they can either be a lifeline drawing us closer to God or a force that pushes us away.

Friendships are like rudders on ships; they might seem a minor part of your life but can steer you in significant directions. Today friendship is often misconstrued as merely agreeing with each other, but true friendships—those ordained by God—challenge you and guide you back to the cross. Whether you are in a crisis or know someone who is, remember that while many may agree with your pain, a true friend helps heal it.

Remember, don't reduce your friends to just people in your comments section or those who don't reciprocate vulnerability. Friendship is where you are known and where you also truly know someone else. Find people who don't just like you when all is well but who know when to stand with you when all is hell.

Own Version of Jesus

I know the phrase "Deconstruction exists because discipleship does not" can be highly offensive. I remember sharing this once and immediately receiving comments from leaders about how I was wrong. They told me I didn't understand the journeys that had led people to deconstruct their faith. While I may not know everyone's story or what each person has endured, I do believe that if we are led into deconstruction, it is most likely not by the Holy Spirit. The Holy Spirit guides us toward life, truth, repentance, humility, love, godliness, peace, fruitfulness, and the other fruits of the Spirit.

I can say this with confidence because I find no instance in the Scriptures, in the life of Jesus or His disciples, where they concluded, "Well, I guess everything must be garbage. I guess this situation is so painful I have to walk away. Let me question everything Jesus has taught me." In fact there were many moments of crisis, loneliness, and even betrayal. Consider Peter at a pivotal moment in John 6:66 when many disciples abandoned Jesus after His controversial teaching about eating His flesh and drinking His blood. Jesus then asked His remaining disciples, "Are you going to leave me too?" (John 6:67, paraphrased). Peter's response, "Lord, to whom shall we go? You have words of eternal life," exemplifies a commitment that sustained him to the end (John 6:68).

I imagine the scene—though I wasn't there—when Peter, perhaps with tears in his eyes, counted the cost of following Jesus, realizing it demanded everything from him. This is the decision faced by those deconstructing: Is Jesus worth everything? The response to this question could determine the path one takes.

Peter easily could have chosen to follow the crowd, and his relationship with Jesus might have become a thing of the past. He could have boasted about all the miracles he witnessed and reminisced about his closeness to Jesus. Likely, Peter would have developed his own view of Jesus, as often happens when you once walked with someone but no longer do. You retain the views, memories, and moments created, but eventually, they remain just memories. It is the continual walking with someone that allows you to truly know them, ensuring they are not merely someone you once knew.

Deconstruction, defined as "the analytic examination of something (such as a theory) often in order to reveal its inadequacy," often harbors a critical spirit.[3] It embodies a desire to prove a point or justify feelings, and sadly, it usually does not lead people back to Jesus but instead to their own versions of Him.

These personalized versions of Jesus might emphasize aspects such as racial equality, social justice, or political engagement, skewing Him to fit personal narratives rather than His own. Remember, the kingdom of God is not a democracy but a theocracy with a King we follow. Those deconstructing may prioritize aspects of Jesus that resonate with them personally, often overlooking His broader teachings. Jesus knew that the solution to issues was not in political revolution but in a revolution of the heart. He aimed to address the darkness that sin had introduced into the hearts of men and was eager to bring them from that darkness into the kingdom of light.

Here's how to determine if you, or maybe someone you know, have created your own version of Jesus:

- Does the Jesus you follow prioritize your feelings over His commands?
- Does He empathize more with your sin than with the redemption His blood provides?
- Does He focus more on cultural relevance than on eternal truths?
- Is He reluctant to offend you or challenge your personal beliefs?
- Does He prioritize your happiness over your holiness?
- Does He promise only prosperity and not suffering?
- Does He suggest some biblical teachings are outdated?
- Is His concern more for your comfort than for carrying your cross?
- Does He resemble a self-help guru more than a Savior and King?

- Does He validate your grievances and choices that are contrary to His teachings?
- Does He downplay the difficulty of denying sin?

If you answered yes to any of these, you might have reshaped Jesus based on your experiences, pains, or events within the church. It might have been easier to create this image than to confront the pain He wished to help you through. Yet there is good news: His mercies are new every morning, and repentance is just a conversation away, no matter how long you've harbored certain mindsets.

Throughout this book you will face many decisions about changes you need to make in your life. You'll need to relinquish old offenses, allow God to heal your pain, and remove bandages you've worn for years, perhaps decades, so that you can continue walking with Him.

It may be easy for you to think, "Oh, that's not me," or to assume this book, this chapter, is meant for someone else because you haven't deconstructed or left the faith. I encourage you to let this chapter act as a mirror. Ask God to search your heart. If you find yourself in a dark place in your faith, remember that the tomb was also dark for three days. You might feel lifeless, but after three days Jesus resurrected. I believe a resurrection is also coming in your faith.

I've never met anyone who became a Christian with an initial desire to abandon Jesus. Instead, I remember their eagerness to leave their old life for something better. A key verse we often forget is, "Restore to me the joy of Your salvation" (Ps. 51:12).

Let's return to a time before you felt pain, before you were offended or hurt by a leader, and before you knew what religion was, when your heart was filled with gratitude for being saved from your sins and old life. Remember why you started following Jesus: His patience, kindness, love, holiness, righteousness, forgiveness, everlasting love, faithfulness, fatherhood, generosity, friendship, nearness, trustworthiness—this list goes on.

When I think about who God is, I don't see reasons to leave Him. Often people leave Jesus for what He is not, or they project their hurts from others onto Him. Jesus is not meant to be the focal point of your pain but the center of your healing. Even for those on the brink of denial, like Peter, Jesus waits on the shore, patient and understanding, ready to restore those who turn back to Him as shown in John 21.

For too long people have let their church experiences dictate their relationships with God. Yet the church, like a biological family, is inherently flawed—comprised of imperfect people following a perfect God. If you're seeking perfection in church, you won't find it in the pews or behind the pulpit; you will find it in Jesus, the One preached about.

Over the years, I've had many reasons to remain hurt or offended, and I wish for forgiveness from those I've wronged. I've faced great doubts and moments of self-righteousness. What I share here are glimpses into my private and public moments with God. I am no better than anyone struggling with their faith. As a preacher of the gospel for over a decade, I know I've never stopped needing Jesus, nor do I need Him any less than anyone else. I am here today not because I've always chosen God but because He has chosen me. In my moments of pain or error, He has always found me.

I'd like to share a story with you about a man I met in 2018 who has become a friend. Many consider him a legend for the bands he's played with, including Korn, and the records he's sold, but I say he's a legend because of his profound dedication to Christ. This is Brian "Head" Welch's story.

Brian "Head" Welch

It's pretty obvious to me that when people leave the faith, in my opinion, their intimacy with Jesus becomes nonexistent, which is very, very unfortunate in my eyes.

Maybe they grew up in church, or maybe faith came later in life. But it was most likely a surface Christianity that was lived out by attending Sunday church with very little Bible study and by failing to gain wisdom about our "oneness with Christ" identity, developing a deep and rich relationship with the Father, Son, and Holy Spirit. I have seen this to be common across many churches and Christians in the West.

In my opinion, if we don't learn and personally discover who we truly are, connected in union with Christ, then any of us can easily fall away at any time. This is the most important issue every single one of us needs to discover. And in my experience it happens mostly by being alone with God, praying, meditating/contemplating (which is being quiet and setting your affections and thoughts on God), and loving Him by worshipping Him through music.

When I was ten years old, I wanted to become a rock star. I started playing guitar and getting better and better at it. Electric guitar was my everything. Since I was bullied a lot, it became my comfort. Fast-forward fourteen years, and I was living in Hollywood and my band, Korn, signed a record deal. We went on to sell over forty million records, becoming one of the biggest metal bands of all time. But I fell into the same traps most rock stars fall into: sex, drugs, and rock 'n' roll. Jesus said, "What does it profit a man to gain the whole world [but lose] his soul?" (Mark 8:36, ESV). And boy, did I lose my soul—I lost who I really was inside. I didn't recognize myself anymore. But thank the Lord I didn't lose myself forever!

In 2005, after twenty years of alcoholism and eleven years battling sex and drug addiction—actually using meth every single day for the last two years of my addiction—I ended up being invited to a church. And when I went home to pray after receiving Christ at church, the glory and love of God poured into my soul. Like many have described, it felt like liquid love pouring into me. I had been high or drunk half of my life up to that point, and here I was sitting at my house after a church service, high on God's glory and love. Before that day, I'd thought Christianity was a complete joke! We can probably all agree some of Christianity *is* a joke, but I found out that very day Jesus was no joke at all! It was the best high I'd ever felt! Every other high from street drugs came with a dark feeling, but this high given by Christ's love was so pure and beautiful. No hangovers!

Truly, the living water of Christ's Spirit filled me that day, and I've never been the same. It's been almost twenty years since that day, and I always tell everyone if it wasn't real, I would've walked away a long time ago. A relationship with Christ is the most real thing I've ever experienced in all my years on this planet!

And when I think about my own failures, done by my own actions, they're horrible sins and failures made by my own choices—falling back into porn, drinking, anger, rage, watching things I shouldn't watch on TV, cursing God out—you name it, I've done it! And isn't it just like God to not be offended. And He'll sit with us in our ugliest form, ready to transform the darkest, most shameful situations into beautiful stories. Behind the scenes God was actually using my mistakes and failures and turning them around to become success stories.

It's just what He does. I have a track record of twenty years where He's done it over and over and over. It doesn't make sense to the natural mind; He's just so good that we can't even comprehend it at first. Nobody on this earth even comes close to how good and incredibly kind God is to us in our weak, distorted, broken human existence. And I will be grateful to Him forever.

I'll never forget having Brian over to our home to eat soup during his forty-day fast. His story is especially meaningful to me because it's one thing for someone who has nothing to follow God but entirely another for someone who has experienced all the world has to offer to choose to follow Jesus, knowing there is nothing greater despite the ups and downs they've encountered.

Every legend in the faith understands this: Christianity is not about humanity reaching up to God but about God reaching down to humanity. Christianity has nothing to do with my own goodness but everything to do with His goodness. My righteousness is not grounded in what I do but in what He did on the cross.

Make It Personal

- Do you find yourself following the cultural Jesus or the biblical Jesus? Are you trying to create a personalized version of Jesus that aligns with your own desires and pain? How might this version differ from the teachings of Jesus in the Bible?

- Have you allowed pain and disappointments to shape your theology of Jesus?

- What specific experiences, if any, have contributed to your own feelings of disappointment or disillusionment with the church or with faith in Jesus?

- What do you deeply long for in your spiritual life? How does this compare with what you've been experiencing in your faith journey?

- How do you reconcile your dissatisfaction with certain aspects of Christianity while maintaining a commitment to your faith?

- What is your understanding of deconstruction? How do you differentiate between questioning your faith and completely abandoning it?

Chapter 2

REDEEMED

In chapter 1 we broke down the reasons for deconstructing and why so many people are leaving the faith. We discussed people leaving the faith or creating their own versions of Jesus. We identified signs that you're leaving the faith and ways to know that you're not following the Jesus of the Bible. But here I want to show you the beautiful things that God makes new when we choose to follow Him out of the tomb.

I have spent the last seventeen years learning daily what it means to be a Christian. My insights haven't come from the places where I've preached, the nations I've visited, the books I've written, the events I've organized, or the schools I've reached. Rather, I've learned that salvation is much more than a prayer—it's an initiation into a life of dying to what I was never meant to be. This dying process involves navigating challenges I never thought possible to overcome, but on the other side of laying down my life, I've found restoration, renewal, and reconstruction. It's a lifelong process where God takes a shattered heart and life and, if we're willing to yield, perfects them until we stand face to face with perfection itself.

Early in my faith I began to experience what persecution feels like—not the kind found in third-world countries but the kind within my own home. I was saved at sixteen, and unlike those who grow up in Christian homes, my early life was marked by brokenness. I was a child born out of wedlock and exposed to things no child should see, leading to a life full of unexpected challenges.

I recall returning home from high school one day discouraged because I was still struggling with issues I thought Jesus would have delivered me from. To top it off, each week, my stepdad would sit with me, insisting that God wasn't real and that I was foolish for believing otherwise. He urged me to be "normal"—to drink, smoke, and engage in sex.

I remember one night in my room after reading the Bible feeling utterly frustrated with where I stood with God and my circumstances. Although I had been saved, nothing externally seemed to have changed. I returned home to the same parents, the same stepdad, and my mom—who is now a strong believer but wasn't back then—and I continued to struggle with many of the same issues. Now, I had Jesus, which sometimes confused me, especially when I heard about others who experienced instantaneous transformations.

While some aspects of my life were transformed immediately, other areas were still undergoing renewal and restoration in my mind. That night, overwhelmed by frustration, I grabbed my heavy Bible and hurled it against the wall of my bedroom while screaming, "God, I can't do this. Why did You save me? It's worse now. I feel like I've tasted freedom that I'll never fully realize."

The days grew darker as I watched my mom endure another divorce after thirteen years of marriage, our stepfather leaving just days before Christmas. We took cold showers that winter, unable to afford heating, and survived on one-dollar spaghetti. My mom struggled to find work after thirteen years as a homemaker, and my siblings wrestled with the pain of their father's abandonment. Temptation to renounce my faith and question God's presence was constant.

Yet these moments forged some of the strongest attributes of my faith today.

What prevents a believer from completely abandoning their faith? Is it more frequent Bible reading, a robust prayer life, or predestination? I believe it's the continual renewal of the mind that sustains us. As I mentioned, although nothing externally changed when I was saved, everything internally did. The Scripture speaks of renewing our minds—a process that enables us to rise each time we fall. How does the righteous man who falls seven times manage to get up again? (See Proverbs 24:16.) It's through a relentless renewal of the mind, a vital practice for every fall and rise.

Believing the Truth

One of the lies the devil will tell you is that to forgive is to show weakness or that allowing the Lord to restore or reconstruct will only lead to more pain. Another deception is the belief that forgiveness means burying or suppressing your pain, but that is far from true forgiveness. You see, forgiveness is the first step in allowing the Lord to reconstruct the broken areas of your life, a topic we will hit on deeper in another chapter. I believe the Lord does not merely recycle old things to make something new; rather, He desires to make all things new again. Restoration, renewal, and reconstruction are integral to God's plan, extending beyond the day of salvation and throughout the life of a believer.

Whenever I read Scripture, I rarely see just black letters on white pages. In my almost twenty years of following Jesus, I have come to understand that the Bible is filled with real men and women. The disciples had real challenges, issues, and emotions, just like any normal human being. Without adding to the Word, I like to imagine the emotions behind it. When I read certain passages, I picture the humanity of those men. I want to look at a story in the Bible that you've likely read but may have never considered in this light. It is a story found in the Gospels of Luke and John.

This is a story about restoration and how great failures, deep sadness, great pain, and even falling away can be completely turned around by the announcement of good news. I want to suggest something controversial, but hear me out: Even though the Bible says that the truth will set us free, I have found that the truth alone does not set anyone free. Instead, the truth provides another option for us—one of freedom.

Let me explain. You've likely experienced moments when you believed a lie, and then the truth was presented to you. If you're truly honest, you might admit that the truth alone could do nothing unless you chose to believe it. Before knowing the truth, all you had was the lie. For someone whose heart has been shattered, who is losing faith, who is on the verge of deconstruction, or who has deconstructed, the first steps to restoration are receiving the good news and embracing the truth.

When the women came to announce what they found at the tomb, they must have startled the disciples as they were mourning. (See Luke 24:1-12.) Their leader, best friend, Savior, and Messiah had been dead for three days. I won't even try to get into the emotions of what that might have felt like. I'll let your mind think for a moment. Not only was someone they were in deep friendship with gone, but I can imagine in those three days a lot of their theology died as well.

How could this man have been the Messiah if He could not raise Himself? Thoughts like, "Why would He leave us?" probably came. For those who witnessed Him on the cross, memories of Him walking on water, healing the sick, and raising the dead were probably questioned as this once powerful Messiah lay beaten and bruised on the cross of Calvary. Depression, anxiety, and deep hopelessness were most likely filling some of the disciples' hearts, along with the fear of being put on a cross themselves as His disciples. They were probably not in the best standing with the religious leaders or the Roman government.

As the women proclaimed that He was not in the tomb and that He had risen, disbelief likely mingled with their grief. The last image they had of Jesus was of Him broken, weak, and defeated. The Scriptures say the disciples did not believe the women at first (Luke 24:11). But John tells us that two ventured to the tomb, about to be astonished by the grand reentrance of their Savior and friend, Jesus (20:3–10).

He was no longer confined to a tomb or hanging on a cross, no longer crowned with thorns. He had risen from a brutal beating, one that no other human could endure, defeating death itself. But before delving into this pivotal moment in human history, let's consider our place in this narrative. While I believe we die with Christ and are raised with Him, I want to focus momentarily on the two disciples who chose to believe—or at least to investigate the tomb as John records. (See John 20.)

We often breeze over this passage, failing to see it as a vivid depiction of restoration. You see, many assume that restoration requires immediate, tangible, physical change, but I contend that it begins when the heart dares to believe again. Can you imagine the courage required for Peter and John to rise from their sorrow and head toward the tomb, choosing to believe amid disbelief?

Scripture does not indicate any reason for the disciples to expect Jesus was alive; this news was their first glimmer of hope in three days. They were literally enduring three days of hell on earth engulfed in silence, yet restoration was on the horizon.

I'm not suggesting that this detail is in the Bible; rather, I'm imagining what that run to the tomb might have looked like. With every step that Peter and John took, drawing ever closer, their hearts were probably racing—only to find the tomb empty. See, restoration for those who have been wounded or are being reconstructed begins by allowing the heart to believe first. It involves trusting in the Word of God, no matter the external circumstances, and believing that as long as there is breath in your lungs, His work in you is not finished.

Restoration begins in the heart and gradually transforms the mind and life. Belief is not just a concept; it is a powerful weapon for the believer and often the first target of the devil's attacks. The enemy will use anything—music, friends, family, and even well-intentioned advice—to sway you from faith, telling you that belief is futile and restoration impossible. He aims to magnify your despair, obscuring your ultimate redemption. Our belief is often the first thing dismantled by the mindsets that lead us to deconstruct or fall away from our faith, or it's the first thing questioned in moments of pain. Just as God can speak to you in many ways, so too can the enemy, who will attempt to lead you away from belief.

The Greek word for *restoration*, *apokatastasis*, encompasses meanings such as reconstitution, restitution, and reestablishment.[1] The beauty of restoration is that it not only returns you to the place you were but also restores everything that was taken from you before that difficult period. It's one thing to lose money and start over to recoup; it's entirely another to begin again and have everything you lost fully restored. For those who feel they have lost years to pits, failures, and lies, take heart—the King is coming to restore it all.

Consider the man's withered hand in Matthew 12:13, which was restored when he stretched it forth. Here's a thought: Imagine this man's hand, devoid of muscles from disuse, suddenly regaining years of muscle tone and returning to its proper shape in mere seconds.

Now, I invite you to pause and reflect. Think about the aspects of your life that have withered your walk with God. Take a moment to offer up these areas to Him, asking for restoration and healing.

Pray this prayer:

> *Jesus, just as You healed the man's withered hand in Matthew 12:13, just as You restored sight and strength in Mark 8:25 and Luke 6:10, I ask You to heal and restore me now. It must have been so hard for that man to stretch out his withered hand using*

> his last bit of strength, but as he did, You restored it. I too stretch out to You the parts of my life that feel withered and broken. Touch them; heal them; make all things new. In Jesus' name, amen.

Take a few moments now to sit with the Lord before continuing to read.

What We Sell Jesus Out For

The things we sell out our Savior for can rob us of our lives, joy, and peace. I'll admit I have been guilty of this many times. I wish I could say I've never taken offense, but that would be untrue. I wish I could claim I've never felt anger toward another believer or people in ministry, whether they hold titles or not, but that too would be dishonest. The truth is, I have repeatedly sold Jesus out for the pain in my own heart and for situations I could not comprehend.

There have been times when I felt like abandoning my faith. Yet by God's grace He has gently drawn me back time and time again. I stand here today as a man who walks with a limp, bearing scars from over a decade of faith, having endured numerous trials and tribulations. The process of reconstruction—deeply biblical and inherently a process of renewal—has been pivotal.

When I talk about selling out Jesus, I don't mean He could be sold for any price, though Judas tried. It means we give up our relationship, our obedience, and our commitment to Him in exchange for worldly gains. I believe every believer has been guilty of this, yet I do not believe it is the path we must take to walk out our salvation and faith.

We've often judged Judas harshly, wondering how he could betray Jesus. What kind of friend does that? He's been depicted in sermons for decades as the epitome of betrayal, with bands even named after him. Judas is remembered not for any good he may have done but for his final act of betrayal—selling Jesus for merely thirty pieces of silver, an amount worth perhaps only $91 to $441 today.[2] That's not even enough to cover rent in the United States.

It's debatable whether we're more upset that he betrayed Jesus or that he did it for such a trivial amount. Nevertheless it's clear he sold out his friend, the Savior, who had supported him through many trials and tribulations. He betrayed someone, for such a meager price, who had walked beside him, loved him, and taught him the way, and would ultimately sacrifice His life on the cross for him.

And although we judge Judas, I believe that in many ways at times we have been Judas. We've sold out our relationship with Jesus for trivial offenses and hardships. We've allowed disagreements in our local church, disputes over hierarchy, and roles within ministries to drive us away from our Savior, costing us dearly.

In every area where we have sold Jesus out, it can be made right. Repentance is the key. Only you are aware of the areas where you have allowed darkness to creep in—even if you're serving in ministry and appear outwardly fine. Yet inwardly, like Judas you may have a sense of entitlement that metaphorically leads you to dip into the money bag of your life and take what you believe is owed to you (John 12:6).

This could manifest as a constant desire for recognition or wondering when it will be your turn to preach. Perhaps you feel your service to God should eventually yield some monetary benefit, as if God and people owe you for your efforts. There might be times when you feel entitled to never be wounded, or perhaps you haven't learned how to correctly perceive when God is working within you through difficult circumstances. Remember, nothing is owed to you; you have paid no price. Christ paid it all. Losing sight of the cost of your salvation might lead you to sell Jesus out to the lowest bidder.

If there is anything we should be selling out, it is our old lives and mindsets. We should sell out the lie that deconstruction is the ultimate conclusion, and we should die to anything that threatens our relationship with Christ. Now let's take a look at the restoration available to us through Jesus.

Restoration

There is massive restoration coming to those who have bitten the lie of deconstruction. Restoration will not be found solely in debates or theological studies trying to determine who is right or wrong. Many forget how long those three days must have felt when Jesus was in the tomb, especially for those who followed Him closely. Their faith was wrecked, their theology shattered, and they were tempted to figure out what God was doing or to find another rabbi to follow.

During those three days, they were in a theological crisis because their Savior and King, who should have triumphantly overthrown Rome, was now dead by Rome's hand. They were in hiding and probably fearing for their own lives. Would you not have felt the same way if your leader and his ministry were being publicly scrutinized by the church and government, and then your leader was put to death? Everything they believed probably began to die with the body of their Savior, as they had a front-row seat to watch Jesus be crucified.

At their lowest—likely with eyes puffy from crying and hearts defeated from the three long nights Jesus spent in the tomb—He rose. His resurrection was not kept a secret. He appeared to His disciples, and the Bible says many others saw Him too. Their shattered theology of the Messiah was corrected by His appearance. I want to say that there is restoration for those who have fallen away, for those who have cried themselves to sleep in disappointment with their faith, and for those who have struggled for answers as to why certain things happened while they were Christian.

A resurrection day is coming, whether in this age or the next. A resurrection is coming to those who feel as though there could be no life after what they've walked through. There is. For the disciples the resurrection of Jesus was a reintroduction to Him. They knew the Jesus who had walked on water, healed the sick, and raised others from the dead. But for the first time they knew the Jesus who was beaten, was put on a cross, died, and resurrected. It was something they had never seen before in their three years of walking with Him.

Reintroduction to Jesus

As I mentioned earlier, reconstructing takes a reintroduction to Jesus. The temptation with this reintroduction is to go back to viewing things the way you did before or trying to find God the way you did before. It could even be tempting to try to re-create scenes or scenarios that replicate moments you met Him before, hoping that if you can re-create the moment, the church service, the moment of reading a verse, or that one worship song where you encountered Him, He will come and meet you as He did. But that would mean He's not alive and that the Jesus you are looking for is just an idol that you can position where you want.

As you get reintroduced to Jesus, you are going to meet Him in ways you've never imagined. The beautiful thing about walking out of pain as a believer is that your love for Christ matures. It's unlike the first day you got saved, when you hadn't been offended yet by anybody in the church because you didn't have the time to be. You'd only been saved a few seconds; you hadn't really been hurt yet by a leader or another brother or sister in the body of Christ. When you walk out of pain, the love you carry for Jesus grows stronger and deeper than the day you accepted Him because that love now has cost you. And Jesus can now appear to you differently. He can lead you differently.

Remember when the disciples didn't recognize Him when He reappeared after the cross? The Bible says He came in another form (Mark 16:12). Those who met a religious, rigorous Jesus in today's generation and those who met a Jesus who simply cares about them following rules but not about them falling in love— those people are going to have a radical paradigm shift when they meet the man who gave it all for them.

There is even a radical shift for those who thought that Jesus abandoned them in their last season. You felt alone and asked yourself, "How can God be good if He's allowed me to go through all that I've gone through?" Jesus is going to come to you, meet you, and show you that where you thought you were alone, you never were. Although when I was young, my mom and dad were not Christians, oddly enough in our hallway growing up there used to be this picture with a famous story that you might have heard of: the "Footprints" poem.[3]

The paraphrased summary is this: there was a man walking with God on the beach. There were two sets of footprints, and when the man went through a hard time, there was only one set of footprints. The man reluctantly asked God why He left him in that season, and God replied, "I never left you." He said, "Well then why is there only one set of footprints?" God said, "That was when I carried you."[4] You may realize as you're reading this book how little you were abandoned by God and how much He actually carried you.

Renewal

The renewing of our minds is vital for reconstruction. Psalm 51:10 exhorts, "Create in me a pure heart, O God, and renew a steadfast spirit within me" (NIV). It's crucial for you to understand that God doesn't recycle; He creates anew. This is what renewing your mind and reconstruction must look like. Life's hardships—pain, trials, betrayals, and tribulations—often shatter the human heart, but remember, God does not patch things up with old pieces. He completely renews, creating all things new again.

Proverbs 4:23 tells us, "Above all else, guard your heart, for everything you do flows from it" (NIV). When God renews us, that purity infuses every aspect of our being. Romans 12:2 challenges us not to conform to the world's ways but to be transformed by renewing our minds, enabling us to discern God's will—His good, pleasing, and perfect will. I would like to further break this down because I believe it forms a foundation for those who have left the faith or are considering leaving, providing a basis for them to rebuild their relationship with God. It also serves as a crucial warning for believers—to guard against falling and being deceived by the many challenges and situations that will inevitably arise.

It doesn't take rocket science to recognize that the world follows a distinct pattern and way of life. The world operates on visible patterns and responses, often endorsed and amplified by social media, that blur the lines between believers and nonbelievers. The Greek word *syschēmatizō*, used in Romans 12:2, suggests being molded into a pattern.[5] However, Jesus' mission was not to adapt to worldly structures but to renew them from the ground up. Thus we face a choice: Conform to the world or undergo transformation.

Our minds being renewed in this hour is our sole path to liberation. The Greek word for renewal, *anakainósis*, signifies a "renewal" or "renovation," a "complete change for the better" achieved by God's power.[6] This concept emphasizes an elevation to a new level—not just a simple restoration of the old but a transformative process that brings about newness. Yet many of us are still grappling with life's challenges, using outdated thinking that remains far beneath where Christ reigns. That's why our results never change, why we continue to encounter the same types of negative communities, and why, no matter how often we switch churches, we end up surrounded by the same types of embittered and angry individuals. Renewing our minds is an essential, God-led process, yet it also beautifully incorporates our active participation. It involves a daily commitment to focus on divine rather than worldly matters.

THE FRUIT OF AN UNRENEWED MIND

There is much at stake if our minds are not renewed—it can cause one to remain deconstructed from their faith. Jesus is all about breaking down old systems. Look at His death—the veil in the temple, which separated man from God, was torn, giving people direct access to the Father. His body, which housed the Spirit of the living God, was broken down to be rebuilt.

Many have had their faith destroyed by religion, hurt, pain, or offenses with ministries or leaders, and they have remained in that place. Maybe they were taught that God deeply cared about their passions, so their Christianity was based on their gifts and how those could be used for God. This has led many young people to believe that God needs them; that belief causes them to go where they feel needed. But they never realize their need for God. This is why we see young people moving from church to church.

I am hopeful for change. Though I haven't been alive long, more than ever I've seen a longing for simplicity where Bible reading and prayer are at the center of believers' hearts in this generation.

Let's examine the mindset of a believer who has not yet experienced the renewing of the mind shown in Romans 12:2.

1. Condemnation

An unrenewed mind often experiences condemnation, a significant foothold in a believer's life. Just as the Holy Spirit speaks within us and sometimes sounds like our own thoughts, the enemy will take advantage of us to whisper lies, bringing about a double-mindedness. Often we believe those lies as if they are our own thoughts, or even worse, we believe they're from God. This is not superstitious; remember, the devil has been deceiving humanity far longer than any of us have been alive. The devil is not a jack-of-all-trades; he is a master of one thing: deceiving humanity into not believing God. He can't stop us from pursuing salvation, but he will do all he can to pervert, pollute, and distort our salvation.

Sadly, I have seen this countless times. Once strong believers become suffocated by offense or various trials. There comes a point when we must acknowledge that the Bible is our manual for faith.

2. Selfishness

Another fruit of a believer whose mind has not been renewed is a selfish Christianity, not a selfless one. Nowhere do we find our Savior, Jesus, to be selfish. In fact if you take every situation you are or were angry about and ask yourself how Jesus would respond, you would probably always find a selfless response. Throughout scripture we see Jesus receive rejection from the religious leaders of His time and skepticism from the people; even those who followed Him closely began to leave (John 6:66). In fact Jesus says in John 6:67, "Do you want to go away as well?" (ESV).

We never see Jesus build an easy-to-join ministry. He never declared people part of God's family before they accepted His message. In fact, He was very upfront about the cost of following Him. Jesus warned of being hated by many, forsaking family, picking up one's cross, denying oneself, and taking nothing on the journey (Matt. 10:22, 35–39; Luke 9:3). He knew a watered-down gospel would have greater long-term costs. These teachings might seem extreme today, but they reflect a deep wisdom and commitment to genuine discipleship.

The primary way for us to rid our minds of selfish Christianity is by renewing our minds and allowing the Word of God to wash us of things we might even fully believe are true. Yes, this may be difficult, but I would like you to repeat this with me: "Christianity is not about me. Every right that I believed I had has been nailed to the cross with Christ. It is Christ that now lives in me." (See Galatians 2:20.)

This is a powerful statement. Christ lives in us, which means that every day He chooses to love and live His life through our skin, eyes, actions, words, and motives. Christianity is no longer about attendance; it's about representation. It's like working for a company—you can't act, talk, or treat people however you want because you represent the company. How much more should this be our approach as Christians representing Christ?

3. Retaliation

Another fruit of an unrenewed mind in a believer is retaliation. This can be a touchy subject, but I feel it is needed in the heightened culture we live in today. Nowhere in Scripture will we find where Jesus says to retaliate against a brother. It cannot exist in the Word because it never existed in the heart of God. Jesus takes a saying that would have been very prevalent in the Old Testament—one that we know far too well: an eye for an eye, a tooth for a tooth—and He totally rearranges it.

Matthew 5:38–42 says, "You have heard that it was said, 'Eye for eye, and tooth for tooth.' But I tell you, do not resist an evil person. If anyone slaps you on the right cheek, turn to them the other cheek also. And if anyone wants to sue you and take your shirt, hand over your coat as well. If anyone forces you to go one mile, go with them two miles. Give to the one who asks you, and do not turn away from the one who wants to borrow from you" (NIV).

Jesus said, "Do not resist." Turning the other cheek has more to do with what's in our hearts than with enabling someone to hurt us. Jesus emphasized in verse 39 that revenge and retaliation would never be the key to responses in moments of pain (Matt. 5). If they were, He would have said, "If someone slaps you on the cheek, slap them back."

The next verse hits on another element of our hearts as Jesus addresses the longing to take revenge not just from physical pain but also from possessions that were stolen (Matt. 5:40). How many believers do we know who, when something is taken from them, retaliate with revenge instead of seeking reconciliation and godliness? Instead of being a godly example, they instantly resort to self-preservation.

Now let's go to the next verse, where He talks about being forced to go one mile but instead going two (Matt. 5:41). Jesus does not allow us to retaliate in situations or agreements that are broken or changed.

I found myself in a situation a couple of years ago where someone owed me money. For months it bothered me because this person was a believer. I thought everything from, "How could he not pay me? This is wrong," to, "Isn't he a man of God? Shouldn't his leaders know so they could bring correction?" But my heart's motive was wrong. Inwardly, I desired retaliation and revenge.

I remember the day I called this brother in the faith and said that I would forgive his debt and that he no longer had to worry about anything he owed me. To honor him, I also told him that I would not share who he was or that he had taken money from me. Tears filled his eyes on the other end of the phone. Rejoicing took place for a few moments and was quickly replaced by repentance and godly sorrow. This experience taught me an important lesson about why the renewing of my mind was important and why retaliation and revenge could never be motives.

Further in this chapter Jesus calls us to love our enemies and pray for those who persecute us so that we "may be children of [our] Father in heaven" (Matt. 5:44–45, NIV). A child of God can be defined by many things, but there are also many things a child of God will not participate in, with revenge and retaliation being central among them.

4. Entitlement

The final fruit of the unrenewed mind that I'll share is entitlement. Entitlement is defined as "the fact of having a *right* to something."⁷ Entitlement causes emotions such as feeling deserving and feeling owed something. We expect special treatment and believe our voice matters most.

For believers entitlement often masks these traits in religion. An entitled believer gathers importance from position and rallies others to a cause of perceived injustices. This individual seeks to be right, not reconciled. I believe entitlement can fuel depression, among other serious issues, within the life of a believer because an entitled life is like an empty hole that no one, not even God, can satisfy.

Entitlement loves to mask itself in many forms and spreads its message through what we call "processing" or "getting something off my chest." But if we truly believed that God is who He says He is, we would know that He hears every whisper, collects every tear, and is never far from us.

Over the last decade entitlement has taken center stage across social media. It has fueled the already out-of-control fire in the body of Christ. I challenge anyone: Show me one good fruit that entitlement has produced. We've all been guilty of it, myself included. But admitting it is not enough; there must be a renewing of the mind to overcome it.

Years ago I attended a special ministry event in another

country. Unfortunately, I was excited not for what God would do but because of my positions and titles. I looked forward to backstage access and meeting Christian speakers and bands. Writing this now feels disgusting, but I'm thankful for the lessons I learned through this.

At the event instead of being brought backstage, I was given a pass to a nice area, but it was the farthest from the stage. I felt a wave of shameful emotions—anger for not sitting closer and shame for feeling angry. My mind was fixated on myself, and I missed many things God did that day. Flying home, I regretted missing a historic moment and promised never to be in that place again.

Entitlement blinds us to the beautiful things God is doing and amplifies our inward complaints. It's a deadly fruit of an unrenewed mind. Entitlement was key in Judas' betrayal. Selling out Jesus for thirty pieces of silver didn't start that night; it started every time Judas dipped into the money bag, taking what he thought was owed to him (John 12:6). But you can be free from this. Jesus can be enough for you.

Each of these issues points back to the necessity of mind renewal. As believers we're called not to merely resist the world's patterns but to embody Christ's transformative power. This isn't about adhering to religious norms but about embodying the radical, countercultural message of the gospel—a message of death to self and resurrection in Christ, who enables us to live out His love and truth in a broken world.

Reconstruction

I believe that reconstruction in the life of someone who has deconstructed is probably going to look a little different than we thought. For many years I heard this Bible chapter preached from the pulpits, and although I always agree with what the

Word of God says, I'm not so quick to jump the gun on someone's interpretation of it.

The Bible verse that I struggled with for many years was John 15—Jesus is speaking and He says that He is the true vine and His Father is the vinedresser. In verse 2 He states that every branch in Him that does not bear fruit He "cuts off" or "takes away" (John 15, NIV, ESV). The phrase "takes away" is the common English translation from the Greek in the ESV, KJV, and NASB versions of the Bible.

When you read that, you might immediately think that surely there is no hope for you or someone you know who has experienced deconstruction or struggled in the faith. It could feel as though His axe is right at the root of your branches, or you might have heard preachers use this verse to talk about how those who don't serve God rightly or serve the church will be cut off.

Here's the good news: The Greek word used in this verse for "takes away" does not mean that God cuts you off or removes you. The Greek word *airō* means to "lift up."[8] Lifting up branches was a common practice for vinedressers. When a tree was not bearing fruit on certain branches, the vinedresser would lift up the branch and raise it on an arbor, a structure that provides shade and rest for the branch, so that it would produce fruit again. In this Bible reference the Father is the vinedresser.

What a completely different picture of restoration: God does not desire to cut us off and throw us away when we aren't bearing fruit. His desire is to lift us up and provide shade and rest. His desire is that in our times of weakness, we would once again become fruitful believers. In fact time and time again, I have seen pastors' kids who have struggled in their walks with God—or even sometimes left the Lord—eventually come back to Him with repentance and love for Jesus. This was the case in my family for many of my relatives who were gang members and were also the children of pastors.

Maybe you've been feeling discouraged that your life hasn't borne the fruit you hoped to see or that you're still in a place where God is restoring you. Don't lose heart. His desire is that you would bear good fruit as a believer. His desire is that when you are weak, He will lift you up.

Who He Is

I've had so many conversations where people have shared their various opinions of Jesus—people who are both flourishing in their relationships with God and also those who are greatly offended in their relationships with God. I've even heard people use Him to justify their actions, both good and bad. But one guiding truth to live by is when describing who Jesus is, none of our descriptions can come from our experiences. They must come from the truth of His nature. Our experiences often can distort the truth of the nature of God. We even develop full theologies at times that are based on our experiences.

As I mentioned in chapter 1, a consequence of remaining in a deconstructed mindset long enough, if you don't fall away, is creating your own version of Jesus that you follow. But also those who aren't deconstructing can create views of Jesus based on their own self-righteousness. Sadly, with over forty-five thousand Christian denominations, everybody thinks they know who He is. There has even been a church split over emphasizing certain aspects of the person of Jesus.[9] We also see believers putting down other believers who don't carry the same emphasis of Jesus' life that they do.

An example of that in our Christian circles would be the missions and prayer communities. One community might say, "We don't pray enough. Jesus was a man of prayer. Mary was at His feet, and Martha worked way too much." And the other group says, "You don't preach the gospel enough. A mandate was given by Jesus to make disciples of all nations."

Now in telling you about who Jesus is, I feel it is most appropriate to not waste any more time on my opinions or my views but to take you directly to the Scriptures. The late Loren Cunningham, founder of Youth With A Mission, was a modern-day legend in the faith and also a friend. He said once that you can find Jesus and who He is in every book of the Bible. Following is one of the greatest messages that Loren spoke about who Jesus is according to the Scriptures. Even while writing this, I feel the Holy Spirit coming into the room as I hear this message of who He is.

Before reading this next part, I want to ask that you do something different. If you're in a crowded area, don't continue reading. But if you're in a place where it can be just you and God, regardless of where you are in your faith—you could be backslidden, on your way there, or fully burning for the Lord—I want you to begin reading this next part out loud. And instead of declaring to Jesus all the areas that are wrong with you, people around you, the church, and so on, I want you to begin to declare to those issues who Jesus is.

Read the following out loud:

> In Genesis, He is the Creator.
> In Exodus, He's the liberator.
> While in Leviticus, He is the High Priest.
> In Numbers, He is the good spy.
> In Deuteronomy, He's the lawgiver.
> In Joshua, He is the conqueror.
> In Judges, He's the righteous judge.
> In Ruth, He's the kinsman-redeemer.
> In 1 and 2 Samuel, He's the second David, better than the first.
> In Kings, He is the King of kings.
> While in the Chronicles, He's the One that keeps the records, including writing your name in the Lamb's Book of Life.

In Ezra, He rebuilds our temples.

In Nehemiah, He's the rebuilder of our walls of protection.

In Esther, He's the King that gives the edict that saves His people's lives.

While in Job, Job discovers that He is Redeemer that liveth. And then Jesus gave him double for his trouble.

In Psalms, He's the object of our worship and praise.

In Proverbs, He's the wisdom of God.

In Ecclesiastes, He's the great preacher.

In the Song of Solomon, He's the lover of our souls.

In Isaiah, He's high and lifted up in the temple. He is also the suffering servant who lays down His life for us.

In Jeremiah, He is the weeping Prophet.

In Lamentations, [He is] the tears of God.

In Ezekiel, He's the bronze One before whom Ezekiel lies as a dead man.

In Daniel, He's the fourth man in the fiery furnace.

In Hosea, He is the faithful husband to an unfaithful wife,

while in Joel, He is the latter revival. There is no revival without Jesus.

In Amos, He is the cascading justice that flows down into the oceans of the world.

He is the judge of all nations in Obadiah.

In Jonah, He's the God of the second chance. He gave us our second chance.

In Micah, He is the One who does justice, but he loves mercy and he walks humbly with His God.

In Nahum, He's not the Lamb; He's the Lion. He's the wrath of God.

In Habakkuk, He is the glory that the knowledge of Him will cover the earth as the waters cover the sea.

[In] Zephaniah, He sings over us with joy.

In Haggai, He's the latter glory, greater than the former, and the shaker of all nations.

In Zechariah, He's the One that cleanses the robes of the high priest because He's worthy, and says to us, "It's not by your might or your power, but it's by my Spirit," saith the Lord.

In Malachi, He brings the generations together: fathers to sons, sons to fathers.

In Matthew, He is the Messiah.

In Mark, He is the supreme commander.

In Luke, He's the Son of Man,

while in John, [He's] the Son of God.

In Acts, [He's] the builder of the church.

In Romans, He's the second Adam, much greater than the first, who brings us to Abba Father.

In 1 Corinthians, He is the love that is greater than faith and hope.

In 2 Corinthians, [He's] the true Apostle.

In Galatians, He's all nine of the fruit of the Spirit.

[In] Ephesians, He's not only the chief cornerstone of the building that He's building but He's also the full armor of God.

In Philippians, it shows Him there emptying Himself of the glories of heaven to leave heaven to come to earth, and then He dies for us on the cross. He's put into a borrowed tomb. And in the meantime hell is rejoicing, and they've got a big party going on when an uninvited guest shows up. And Jesus takes the keys of death, hell, and the grave, and then God highly exalts Him above every name, that at the name of Jesus every knee will bow, every tongue confess, that Jesus is Lord to the glory of God the Father.

In the Book of Colossians, He's not only the Creator but He's the One that holds the world together.

In the Book of 1 Thessalonians, He's like the mother

nursing the child or father caring for the child—He's both.

In 2 Thessalonians, He's the coming King. Yes, He's coming again, but this time as King of kings and Lord of lords.

In 1 Timothy, He's the one Mediator between God and man.

In 2 Timothy, He's the multigenerational God—the grandmother, the mother, and Timothy.

In Titus, He's the One that cleanses the church.

In Philemon, He frees the slave, and we are those slaves that have been freed by the blood of Jesus.

In Hebrews, He's the rest of faith and the author and the finisher of our faith.

In James, He is our good works without which faith is dead.

In 1 Peter, He says, "Cast your cares on Me. I care for you."

In 2 Peter, He's gracious.

In 1 John, He says, "If you'll confess your sins to Me, I'll be faithful and forgive your sins and cleanse you from all unrighteousness."

In 2 John, like the mother caring for the children, He's a good pastor.

In 3 John, He's also the One sent of God, a missionary who also takes care of the strangers who are missionaries.

In Jude, He warns us of the three false prophets. In every generation they are there. But He is the glory, He is the majesty, He is the dominion, and this spills over into the last book of the Bible.

The Revelation of Jesus Christ, who overcomes the enemy, who overcomes the Antichrist. And we overcome by the blood of the Lamb, Jesus, and the word of our testimony, and loving not our lives even unto death.[10]

What We Say Yes To

After hearing who Jesus is and where He could be found all throughout the Bible, I feel it most appropriate to have a moment where we recommit ourselves to Jesus again. No, I'm not talking about repeating another salvation prayer, I'm talking about recommitting in your heart to follow Him with everything that you have. I heard once from someone that in today's generation we don't like calling sin *sin*; we call it brokenness. But brokenness doesn't need a Savior; a sinner needs a Savior. And Jesus is not called to be our therapist but our Savior and our Lord.

The Bible says that we are no longer slaves to sin but slaves to righteousness. We are no longer victims of Adam's decision in the garden. We are victors because of Jesus' decision on the cross. I want to be up front with you about what you are saying yes to. I've seen some altar calls where the preacher did not fully disclose what individuals were saying yes to when they accepted Christ, and they did not fully know whom they were choosing to follow. So let me make it very clear for you now. Here's what you are saying yes to:

- You are saying yes to a life sold out to Jesus where He is not just your Savior but also your Lord (Mark 10:29–30).

- You are saying yes to picking up your cross and denying yourself (Matt. 16:24).

- You are saying yes to following Him daily (Matt. 16:24).

- You are saying yes to embracing trials and tribulations of many kinds, knowing that He will never leave you or forsake you (Jas. 1:2; Heb. 13:5).

- You are saying yes to true repentance, which is *metanoeō* in Greek and means to do a one-eighty from your life of sin to a life following the cross (Acts 3:19).[11]

- You're saying yes to living for obedience and pleasing the Lord more than for the acceptance and approval of man (Gal. 1:10).

- And ultimately you are saying yes to falling in love with God and letting Him love you because when you love God, you will obey His commands (John 14:15).

Maybe you've been on the verge of leaving the Lord or know someone who fits this description. May this help you put language to the ways you might have felt. I want to say this: Someone who has accepted Christ may try to not go to church, to not read, to not pray, or even to ignore the voice of conviction in their life, but deep down they know they cannot shake the reality of the relationship they once had. Once we've experienced His goodness, we can't pretend it doesn't exist, even if we try to say we've never seen it.

It's like a relative whom we no longer speak to or who we even go so far as to say is dead to us. Just because we say this doesn't change the reality that they are still alive. You might have taken a million steps away from God, but you're only one step away from coming back. Those who have become legends in the faith are not those who have never wrestled with ups and downs in their faith or who have never had great moments of doubt, doubt even in God's existence. They are the ones who have wrestled with these moments and come out on the other side leaning on their beloved Jesus (Song of Sol. 8:5).

Make It Personal

- Have you ever sold Jesus out for something else? If so, what did you prioritize over your relationship with Christ?

- In what ways have your perspectives or thought patterns shifted as a result of reading this chapter?

- How have your thoughts and attitudes impacted the results, or fruit, in your life? Can you identify areas where unhelpful or negative thinking has influenced your actions and outcomes?

- How do you personally perceive forgiveness? Do you see it as a strength or a weakness? How has this perception influenced your ability to forgive others and yourself?

- In what areas of your life do you feel broken or in need of reconstruction? How open are you to the idea that God can not only restore but make these areas completely new again?

- Reflect on a time when you were presented with a truth that contradicted a lie you believed. How did accepting or rejecting that truth impact your life and your faith journey?

- How have your personal experiences shaped your understanding of Jesus? Can you identify any ways in which your view of Him might be influenced by these experiences rather than the truth of His nature as revealed in Scripture?

Chapter 3

OFFENDED

I'VE NEVER MET a believer who woke up desiring to be deceived or to desert their faith for lies. The Greek word for *deceived* is *exapataó*, which can be translated as bamboozled, duped, or "beguile[d]."[1] This is exactly what offense does—it bamboozles believers, tricking them into believing things that distance them from their belief in God. Or perhaps more dangerously it allows them to believe in God without truly believing God. We are called to navigate through life's challenges without succumbing to offense.

Offense is rarely just an initial reaction; more often it serves as a secondary defense mechanism. It shields our pride and covers areas that God wants to address within us. As we know from Proverbs 16:18 and Proverbs 3:34, pride comes before a fall and God opposes the proud. Pride, protected by offense, is not something God designed for us. Instead, there is an invitation to adopt meekness and humility.

In this chapter I will provide tools to help you navigate the offenses you may encounter in various areas of life, including disagreements with family and friends, workplace conflicts, frustrations about where you are versus where you think you should be, and challenges within the church and ministries. As we address these offenses, several transformations can occur. You will learn to embody the scripture, "Blessed are the meek, for they shall inherit the earth" (Matt. 5:5, ESV). True meekness cannot coexist with offense. This transformation will also help you lose a critical eye toward your fellow believers and foster a spirit of grace, mirroring the grace God has extended to you.

Reflecting on an impactful moment, I recall scrolling

through Instagram and hearing Michael Koulianos deliver a sermon that seemed meant not just for me but for our generation. His message about the destructive power of offense struck a chord, underlining how offense can thwart our destinies.

Our cultural climate, particularly among millennials and Gen Z, is saturated with offense. We see divisions—over political views and pandemic responses, and even within denominational lines—often escalating into the formation of new denominations out of these disputes. More concerning is the trend over the past decade, particularly in the past three to five years, of publicly airing grievances. I have even seen individuals justify this behavior by twisting Scripture, claiming that this is what the apostles did. However, this comparison fails unless one is also living a life fully aligned with the apostles' sacrifices and godliness.

The escalation of sharing personal offenses on social media has turned these platforms into arenas where offenses are aired for validation rather than healing. This public sharing does not foster resolution but instead validates our grievances without offering the healing we truly need.

It's crucial to recognize that while it may feel satisfying to share our hurts with a wide audience, this approach seldom leads to genuine resolution or peace. Instead, it deepens divisions and entrenches us in bitterness. When we air our grievances without first seeking God or confiding in a trusted spiritual mentor, we are not aiming to resolve these issues internally but rather retaliating against those we believe have wronged us. This approach harms not just our relationships but our own spiritual health and the broader community's well-being.

We must recognize that information is never neutral. Consider Psalm 1:1, which teaches, "Blessed is the man who does not walk in the counsel of the wicked, nor stand in the path of sinners, nor sit in the seat of scoffers." This verse illustrates that

Offended

listening to ungodly counsel inevitably leads one to stand with sinners and sit among scoffers. We can see that offense, if not dealt with, leaves a body trail of people it affects.

I was struck by a message from Michael Koulianos that I encountered on Instagram, which is relevant to our discussion on offense. He asserts, "If you quit early on God's process—your fault. If you become offended—your fault. Do you know what the word 'offended' means? Trapped. The Greek word is *scandalo*, and it's where we get the English word 'scandal.' You embrace an internal scandal because you believe lies, and they destroy your destiny."[2]

Reflecting on this, you might ask, "How could it be your fault if you're hurt by circumstances beyond your control?" Yet remember 1 Corinthians 10:13, which reassures us that no temptation has overtaken us except what is common to humanity; God is faithful and will provide a way out in every situation, including when we feel offended. You see, the Bible does not claim we won't face challenges, but it does assure us that in every situation there will always be a way out. This promise includes an escape from any current offenses we might encounter, as outlined in that very verse.

Offense has ensnared many, trapping them in a cycle of replaying painful scenarios repeatedly. You might sit there, dwelling on past conversations and text messages, convinced of your righteousness and the other person's faults. As Scripture says, this sort of heart does not allow you to see the plank that is in your own eye because you're so consumed with the splinter that's in the other person's eye (Matt. 7:3). You become entangled in the scandal of offense. Your heart grows weary from the relentless fight to be right, rather than surrendering to the Lord. In this state, with a weakened heart, offense becomes the loudest voice you can hear.

Offense in those moments may feel as close to you as the Holy Spirit. It speaks to you, it leads you, but unlike the Spirit, you are led by offense, guided by your flesh. Being led by your flesh means allowing your mind, your will, and your emotions to dictate your outcomes and responses. Just as the Holy Spirit empowers you to act in accordance with God's will, offense empowers your flesh to commit sin. Think about it; how often have you acted in anger? How many have you seen coming from broken homes or failed relationships finding themselves mired in sin?

I have known individuals who, in a moment of intense anger and offense, committed the unthinkable—taking the life of another or their own. This might seem extreme, and you may think, "That will never be me." Yet undoubtedly they believed the same about themselves. This highlights the dangers of offense. It propels a person further than they wish to go and demands more than they are willing to give. Offense justifies your flesh and your sin, and when it's time to pay up, it presents you with the bill: "For the wages of sin is death..." (Rom. 6:23).

In the second half of the video Michael elaborates, saying the term *scandalo* describes "somebody walking through the woods on a trail, on the right path, but they fall into a trap they couldn't see. If you want to thwart the destiny of God on your life, get really offended."[3]

Offense does not discriminate. It does not care if you hold a title or not, about your economic status, your race, or your religious denomination. Offense cuts deeper, targeting the innermost parts of a person. As Jesus so powerfully stated, it's not what goes into a man that defiles him but what comes out of him (Mark 7:15).

Later in this chapter I'll explore further insights Michael Koulianos shares in this clip that struck a chord with me: One of the gravest traps occurs when you "start to surround yourself with other people who are offended. You cannot walk in truth if you're living in offense."[4] This cannot be overstated: Advice from someone who is offended is compromised. It's like a meal sprinkled with just a bit of poison—no matter how small the dose, poison is deadly. Offense works the same way. I'll also show you how to discern when you are among those who are offended, ensuring you can navigate away from such influences.

Tools to Navigate Current Offenses

When dealing with offense, it is essential to view everything through the scriptural lens. James 1 instructs, "Consider it all joy, my brethren, when you encounter various trials, knowing that the testing of your faith produces endurance. And let endurance have its perfect result, so that you may be perfect and complete, lacking in nothing" (vv. 2–4). The Bible does say "when [we] encounter various trials," and not various offenses, but I don't think many would argue that trials propose great opportunities for great offenses.

The Bible never directs us to become offended. You will not find a passage where God, His Son, or the Holy Spirit permits us to harbor offense. The Holy Spirit does not condone sitting in offense or spreading grievances about your brothers and sisters. You must not confuse the promptings of your flesh with those of the Holy Spirit. The Bible does not say that trials won't come; instead, it promises that they will. However, it also gives us a tool for viewing these trials: "Consider it all joy," it says (Jas. 1:2).

In 2022 I was deeply moved by a story from my local church, UPPERROOM Dallas. A family invited me to pray for their son, who was fighting for his life—a situation that had quickly garnered attention throughout our church and across social media.

As I walked into the hospital room to pray for him, I expected to be greeted by his father—a man somber, upset, distraught, and a mess. But to my surprise I encountered the opposite. If you had met this man at that time, you would never have guessed the depth of his trial. With more faith than I've ever heard in anyone's voice, he spoke of his son's impending healing. Tragically, shortly after our meeting his son passed away.

The same man who had earlier greeted me maintained his smile even in grief. Though he never spoke explicitly about offense, his life was a profound lesson. It demonstrated how, even in the face of the most unimaginable parental nightmare, one can keep their heart, emotions, and thoughts surrendered to the Holy Spirit. This brings me to the first set of tools for overcoming offense: joy and endurance.

The Tools of Joy and Endurance

Joy, if you were unaware, has nothing to do with your emotions—that's happiness. Being joyful is a state of being; it's a mindset. Joy allows us to undergo tests without allowing offense to penetrate our hearts. When tested, maintaining joy rather than succumbing to offense produces endurance. This endurance, in turn, renders us complete, lacking nothing. Unlike joy, offense will consistently highlight what you lack rather than what you possess, and it especially blinds you to the most important presence in your life: Jesus.

What does it mean to have endurance as a believer? It means your faith isn't limited to Sundays or merely a few youthful years before being forgotten in old age. A believer's endurance spans from the decision to follow Christ on Earth to their final breath, as they enter His presence. As the Bible says, "to be absent from the body [is] to be present with the Lord" (2 Cor. 5:8, KJV).

Following Jesus at a young age, to be honest, is not particularly impressive to me. When I encounter a young person who appears passionate about God, I'm seldom impressed. My reaction isn't one of awe at their early devotion, as most young people don't have much to lose. However, when someone has been following Jesus for decades, they develop something called endurance. This endurance is what turns a young person's knowledge into wisdom.

Older generations carry something that should be treasured as gold. They carry endurance. They have gone through enough of life, yet they still remain close to Jesus. When you get around them, there is a residue on their lives that they have been with Him. A lot of times I meet older people with various illnesses who seem to have untouchable joy and gratitude. Their joy and gratitude are not something they cultivated by hearing a sermon one time or listening to a few podcasts. It was by repeatedly choosing God and choosing to not get offended in the midst of hardships.

The Tools of Thankfulness and Gratitude

A couple of other tools that are often overlooked are thankfulness and gratitude. Romans clearly states, "For even though they knew God, they did not honor Him as God or give thanks, but they became futile in their speculations, and their foolish heart was darkened" (1:21). I encourage you to continue reading that chapter in its entirety, but I will pause here for a moment.

Thankfulness and gratitude are mighty weapons in the hands of a believer who has become offended. It is as if you are in a steel cage that is locked. Thankfulness and gratitude are as powerful as if someone handed you the very key to the lock. Additionally, the beautiful aspect of thankfulness and gratitude is that they do not require any external changes for you to possess them. This means you can remain grateful even if your family situation remains the same, your economic status is unchanged, you have not yet received physical healing from God, or you are still dealing with issues in your heart concerning another person. None of these situations have the power to strip away thankfulness and gratitude.

Though similar, your thankfulness and gratitude are quite distinct. Gratitude is when your feelings and emotions show deep appreciation, regardless of the circumstances you are facing. Thankfulness is the expression of inward gratitude outwardly. I believe it is significant when a believer worships God in their heart. However, I also think gratitude reaches another level when they can lift their hands and shout for joy with thankfulness.

You might find it nearly impossible, but with the Lord it is indeed possible to be grateful and not grow offended, even when your calling seems to be disintegrating or even when those who call themselves believers commit heinous acts. You can remain thankful even if the very nation and place where God has called you currently threatens your life. This is the story of my friend, Heidi Baker. I have asked her to share it with us. I pray that it will touch your heart and stir you toward deeper gratitude in your journey. This is the story of my friend and missionary Heidi Baker. I have asked her to share it with us. I pray that it will touch your heart and stir you toward deeper gratitude in your journey.

Heidi Baker

Rolland and I have been privileged to live in Mozambique since 1995. Eight years after we arrived, we moved to the far northern province of Cabo Delgado. It was beautiful, sparsely developed, and largely unreached by the gospel. We were overjoyed to go, and before long God allowed us to witness an extraordinary spiritual outpouring among the tribes there. The Holy Spirit moved in great power. The deaf were hearing; the blind were seeing; the crippled were walking. There were countless baptisms. Other ministers began to pour in, helping us sow and build. We opened a school, and soon we had more than five hundred student missionaries with us. The road ahead looked smooth.

The terror attacks struck us without warning. A rebel group calling itself Al Shabab—who now identify as ISIS—descended suddenly on towns and villages all over the province. They were militantly anti-government and anti-Christian. They tortured, abducted, and murdered many civilians, targeting churches with special hatred. They burned down farms and houses. They drove away the authorities. Within days the government was asking us to evacuate. All of our international students had their visas canceled. In less than forty-eight hours most of our long-term missionaries had to depart as well. We went from seventy-two missionary staff members down to less than a dozen overnight. The pain of having to send away so many of our closest friends and coworkers was intense. We came home from our many airport drives to empty, unused buildings and cried.

For those few of us who could stay, there was great temptation to be offended at God. We might have been overcome with anger that He would allow this. We might have been resentful because all our hopes seemed to have been cut short and all our work blown to pieces. For a while we did our share of complaining! But we quickly decided to pray through the psalms of David—pouring out our grief before Him without trying to hide. We were really honest about how painful it was. Though we were hurting, though most of us had never before experienced such a sudden and traumatic change in circumstances, we genuinely felt that the Lord called us to worship together despite all of it.

I believe that the Lord kept us from bitterness by giving us grace to pour all our distress into worship. We let ourselves weep freely but not for a very long time. In order to step away from anger and offense, we had to focus our eyes on the Lord, on the beauty of Jesus and all that He has done for us. We recognized that in this world we are not entitled to all we might want. The Bible warns us that nations will shake, and there will be wars and rumors of wars, and earthquakes and floods and much more besides. (See Matthew 24:6–7.) This was not the first persecution to fall on His people. It will not be the last. But in all times and through everything, we can find His peace in worship. Heaven is our home, our true reward, and we can taste it now when our hearts are turned toward Him.

For me there was an even more personal moment of struggle when the attacks of Al Shabab continued to intensify. Most of the other missionaries had been forced away. It was during the vivid blood moon of May 2022. Al Shabab had just finished a period of fasting. Local witch doctors were out drumming in their rituals. Tens of thousands of displaced people were fleeing the terror attacks, into our little city of Pemba. I was sitting outside my house in the evening, exhausted, looking up at this huge, bright red moon when I received an incredibly rare phone call from some old and dear friends. These friends had almost never called me before—they were the kind of people who preferred to talk in person. But that night they told me, "The Lord really spoke to us. You need to leave Mozambique immediately. Now. You need to leave Pemba."

To tell the truth, at first I was a little offended with everyone involved. I felt as if I was being asked to leave my calling. My place. But after the call ended,

I looked down at my phone and discovered a lot of new messages. I am part of a group of intercessors on WhatsApp, and there were strings of messages from twelve different people, all telling me that I had to leave immediately. Each one of them said it was urgent. It was an overwhelming amount of warning.

None of this was what I wanted to hear. I said, "Well, I want to hear for myself from the Word of God."

So I did a very Pentecostal thing. I went and opened my Bible to see what the first verse my eyes fell on would be. It was Ezekiel 12:3: "Therefore, son of man, pack your belongings for exile and in the daytime, as they watch, set out and go from where you are to another place" (NIV).

That was the last straw, though I still didn't like it. I decided to surrender and obey all these warnings. It was tremendously difficult because if I left, I wasn't completely sure I'd be allowed back into the country. Things were so dangerous that visas and permits were uncertain. But I packed my things and went.

What I hadn't realized is that one of our national pastors, a man I had worked with for fifteen years but who had recently fallen into scandals with power and money and women, had actually fallen much further than we understood. After I had gone, it came to light that he had been trying to sell me to Al Shabab. He had been in touch with them, seeking to arrange a time and price to lead them to me and have me killed. If they had gone through with it, it would probably have left very few missionaries in the region for a long time to come.

The last of this information came to our attention months later, while I was away in America. During that time this fallen pastor learned that he was dying of AIDS. He repented a short time before he passed away. It was not until this threat to my life had been exposed and resolved that I felt released to go home to Mozambique again. There were no visa difficulties. Those were hard months of waiting, but over and over again, I felt God's constant calling not to be bitter but to turn to Him in worship daily.

During this season I was at a church conference, and I heard a pastor speaking about forgiveness. At first I glossed over the message a little, thinking that I had forgiven everyone in my life. I had forgiven members of my family; I had forgiven my parents. I had forgiven many things large and small over the years. But suddenly I felt God asking me if I would forgive Al Shabab for their violence and terror. That caused a moment of intense pain. I knew I needed supernatural help. I put my hand on my own heart and cried out, "Please, I can't put love in my own heart. I can't take away all the pain. I can't put love in my heart for Al Shabab."

The power of the Holy Spirit hit me in a way I will never forget. He showed me that the fighters of that terror group had so many broken boys, lost and in terrible need. I don't know how many of them will repent in this life, but by a supernatural miracle God did give me love for them. We pray for them now, just as we pray for their victims. Our enemy is not flesh and blood. We overcome our true enemies only with God's love.

God has been merciful to us, and our work was not wiped out. We remain in Cabo Delgado, and despite some continuing violence the church in the north only grows. As often as we have feared for our lives, God has preserved us and done many miracles even in times of sorrow and persecution. Each week there are more baptisms. Our schools grow, we dance, we worship, we sing, and we preach. God is good; our hope is stronger than ever, and to this day we are burning with gratitude because His favor is eternal.

Fruits of Overcoming Offense

Let's discuss what it looks like to overcome offense. There will indeed be fruit. So how do you recognize when you're walking in the fruits of overcoming offense? Because truly overcoming offense shows in noticeable ways. You may have encountered individuals who claim they're no longer offended or insist they've moved on. But everything in their tone and body language says the opposite. The words they speak, their language choice, the way they roll their eyes, and how their demeanor changes all externally indicate something different from what they claim to feel internally.

Over the past decade I've worked with many people, helping them navigate through various situations. Here are a few indicators that you are genuinely bearing the fruits of someone who has overcome offense:

- You can find God's mercy in your life in the person you were offended by.

- You might not see eye to eye with the person you were offended by, but it doesn't mean you can't see Jesus in that individual.

- You can see the best in the person you were offended by and no longer prejudge their motives or actions through the lens of your pain.

- You don't avoid the person you were offended by when you see them, but you can joyfully have conversations with them.

- When you look at the person you were offended by, you no longer see their mistakes; instead, you see a son or a daughter of God.

- You speak well of the person you were offended by when they're not in the room.

- If anybody wants to speak negatively of the person you were offended by, you will be quick to defend them, speaking only what Jesus would speak of them.

The fruit of someone who is no longer walking in offense is them walking in what Scripture calls meekness. Meekness is not a weakness. It is actually strength at its prime. We know that the meek will inherit the earth (Matt. 5:5), and you may wonder what that means. Does it mean God will give you a state or country to rule over? No. But meekness in this age will determine what God entrusts you with in the next. We have to remember that as believers eternity must be at the forefront of our minds at all times. This earth is not our final destination or our home.

As you walk no longer offended, you will also begin to notice the critical eye you once had, and finding faults in your brothers and sisters will begin to clear up. You will no longer have your eyes when you see them, but God's. You will find your heart becoming full of grace, compassion, and mercy. You will find yourself caring more for that person's soul and their eternity than just caring for and focusing on things in the natural. I hope you can see how much is at stake when you bite the bait of offense.

Biblical Examples

I often ponder the countless men and women in the Old Testament who could have been offended at God. Consider

Noah, who endured ridicule for building an ark on dry land. Consider Abraham, informed at nearly ninety that his wife would soon give birth, and the testing of his faith when he was asked to sacrifice his son Isaac, the child of promise. Reflect on Moses, who was commanded to return to Egypt, the very place he had escaped. Then there's Job, who lost everything when God allowed Satan to test him. That's just the Old Testament. Let's delve into the New Testament in a moment.

How about Mary, whose destiny wasn't to become a celebrated evangelist? She didn't dramatically declare her readiness to serve with a cry of "Here I am; send me" at a grand altar call. Rather, her affirmation to God's call cost her everything. She wasn't bestowed a title amid applause; instead, she was given a crying baby. Far from being honored in a synagogue, she found herself on the verge of divorce (Matt. 1:19). Mary's vocation was unlike any other in the Bible; it is a testament to a woman whose fidelity was rewarded by the responsibility to carry what she must have felt was beyond her worthiness (Luke 1:38).

Carrying divinity within her humanity, Mary's days and nights were consumed with the care of the child within her. This period represents one of the most selfless acts any human can perform, completely devoted to the well-being of another. And amid those long nights Mary likely wrestled with many questions about her life and the extraordinary path she was chosen to walk.

The legend of Mary, the mother of Jesus, is often misunderstood. While many praise her primarily for birthing the Son of God, I believe her true legendary status comes from how she carried Him for those nine months. Scripture may not detail what she did during this time, but having observed many women enduring pregnancy, we can infer that it was a time of immense pressure and endurance. Those months involved enduring sleepless nights, managing emotional fluctuations, and undergoing significant physical changes—none of which were about her but entirely about the life she was nurturing inside her.

If that isn't enough, consider Mary's journey after carrying this child through what might have been an emotionally turbulent period—a common experience for many pregnant women. Now she found herself beside Joseph, pondering deeply in her heart. She might have wondered why God led her to give birth to His Son in an area where there was no proper place for His birth. Couldn't God have arranged even a simple lodging for His Son? After hours of searching for a safe place, while fleeing from a king determined to kill her child, Mary surely had to conquer significant internal challenges to prevent offense from taking root.

And then she was in labor. The contractions were likely just as intense despite the child being the Son of God. No matter how severe the pain, her assurance lay in this belief: If God had placed this baby in her womb, then He would see His plan through to its fulfillment. As labor concluded and baby Jesus lay in her hands, that first moment as a mother with her child must have felt surreal as she gazed into the eyes of Jesus.

If you can recognize the magnitude of this woman's legacy from all this, then consider these final thoughts: What made Mary a legend was not just giving birth but her entire journey—from conception to the death of her Son. Mary trusted God completely, despite likely experiencing moments of doubt, fear, and unbelief. She managed well what she was entrusted with, not swayed by public opinion or ceasing her commitment after Jesus' birth. She raised Him in such a way that by age twelve He was found in His Father's house (Luke 2:42-49). This speaks volumes about a mother who instilled truth profoundly into her Son.

It also highlights that Mary did not harbor offense. This became one of her most notable virtues. Her commitment to God was visible and impactful, resulting in a son, Jesus, who in

His teenage years had already developed a personal relationship with His Father. Mary's story and courage exemplify a woman who embraced God's call without any foresight of the outcomes. Even at the death of her Son, there is no suggestion that she harbored any resentment toward God. And at the ascension, whether she witnessed it or not, Mary's heart had likely reached a place of peace and understanding. Her legacy, woven with trust and faithfulness from a young age, shows that Mary didn't just become a legend at her death. She became a legend the moment she gave God her yes.

Ways to Know if You *Are* Offended

You may wonder, "How do I know if I'm offended by people, situations, or even the very calling God has given me?" Before I list ways to know if you are walking in offense, I suggest that offense has a distinctive smell to it—often, like bad breath, everyone else can smell it except you. Here are a few ways to know you are walking in offense:

- Do you constantly complain about people, situations, or circumstances?
- Are you constantly examining God's work in other people's lives and unable to appreciate what He is doing in your own?
- Do you think that you have a better plan than God?
- Do you listen to sermons and messages and think it would be amazing if this other individual heard it, but are unable to see how it could relate to you?
- Do you always find yourself as the victor or victim in every story?

- Does someone else's success in God bother you?
- Are you unsatisfied with what God has given you, and do you covet what He has given someone else?
- Do you only listen to the voice of God and not sound leaders in your life?
- Do you constantly feel better than those around you and think that you're paying more of a price than they are in following Jesus?
- Do you use someone else's actions against you as an excuse to not live out the Bible?

Ways to Know You Are *Not* Offended

As I've just pointed out some ways to know you are offended, there are probably many more that could be on that list. But I now want to point out ways to know that you've really overcome offense:

- You are able to bless and celebrate people around you, whether they are your close friends or even people in other ministries who are doing work similar to yours.
- You trust God's plan for your life even when it has many highs and lows and doesn't go as you planned.
- You are able to receive even from people you've had disagreements with, knowing that the same Holy Spirit that's in you is in them.
- You see others as better than yourself.

- You take ownership of the areas in your life that you need to grow in, and you don't blame your parents, your siblings, your church, your pastors, or your friends for actions you've taken or ways that you need to grow.

- You hold no record of wrong against your brother or sister (1 Cor. 13:5).

- Your heart has been purified; therefore you are able to see God even in the hardest situations (Matt. 5:8).

- You can accept and receive the call of God on someone's life regardless of their past.

Ways to Tell When You're Surrounded by Offended People

As I mentioned before, getting advice from anyone who is offended, whether their offense is great or small, is like being fed by someone who puts a little bit of poison in your meal. It naturally will affect you. Here are a few things that I think will be helpful as telltale signs of offended people:

- There is constant gossip about others in the name of processing or prayer requests.

- There is an undertone of tension about others or other ministries.

- They speak highly of themselves and where God has placed them by putting down everyone else and the places where God has people.

- They are above receiving from anyone.

- They criticize every message they hear and point out every single flaw they can find in the message.

- They desire for their opinions of others to become your opinions of others, as misery loves company.

- There is a constant dissatisfaction with who God is in their lives.

- They blame other people for their current state in their walk with God. It may sound something like this: "Well, if that church or that leader had not done this to me, I would be in a very different place."

- They know enough Scripture taken out of context to be dangerous but not enough to lead people to a transformed life.

- They speak about people who are not in the room to defend themselves.

- They never seem to find fault in their own lives or in situations that have occurred between them and others.

The freest part about not being offended is that instead of taking things into your own hands, you let God take things into His hands. This is hard a lot of times because our humanity demands what we think is immediate justice. It's normal that we see things from our perspective, not seeing things from God's view. There have been many times when I have blessed people who have cursed me. I have monetarily blessed people who have spoken badly of me. And every time I did, I realized that those moments were more for me than they were for them.

If offense does not die in your life and you do not put it on the cross, it will inevitably kill you and your faith. Every legend in the faith has to die to offense. Do not be shocked if, while you're reading this chapter, the Lord calls you to forgive some people or to let some situations go into His hands. Do not be surprised if the Holy Spirit tells you to delete certain posts you've put up or to reconcile with some people you've been at odds with.

Remember that verse that says if you go to the altar and remember that your brother is offended with you, you are to leave your offering and go make it right with your brother (Matt. 5:23–24)? If we lived that verse well, we would see revival. The Bible doesn't say if *you're* offended, but it says if you know your *brother* is offended by *you*. God desires pure hearts more than your offering to the Lord at the altar. Don't let offense rob you any longer.

Offended with Yourself

The last offense I want to address is the offense we hold against ourselves. It's surprisingly common for us to acknowledge God's love and forgiveness for others while struggling to accept the same for ourselves. I've often encountered this, especially in leadership roles where there's an expectation that we should have it all figured out by now. You might find yourself wondering why you continue to wrestle with the same challenges, forgetting that our growth in grace and mercy isn't something we age out of. It's all too easy sometimes to forget that we are not meant to harbor offense, not even against ourselves. I invited my friend Aaron Smith to share his compelling story about a period when he harbored offense against himself.

Aaron Smith

I had done it again...and all I felt was sick, like on the inside there was a goo that I just couldn't get rid of. No matter how hard I tried, I couldn't get clean. I couldn't get the stain I felt on the inside removed. The goo felt permanent. The worst part? I knew better. I had been a Christian for several years at this point. I was a ministry school student and served at my local church. I had been asked to be on leadership teams and speak at youth ministries. That outward appearance of purity was shining bright, yet no one knew on the inside I was wrestling.

My conscience was condemning me, and shame was a close friend. No matter how many times I deleted apps, put a lock on my internet browser, or even tried to quote the Bible to myself, I found myself dominated by a sin that I was told had been dealt with at Calvary. For years I had heard that by the blood of Jesus, I could be free from the power of sin. From an outside perspective my perceived confidence would have told you I was free, but on the inside I needed the gospel. I needed to encounter the man whose zeal hadn't yet touched my life.

Just hours after I responded to an altar call to give Jesus everything, I was once again falling victim to temptation. Pornography was the chain around my neck that seemed to grow increasingly unbreakable. This moment was no different from all the others. Convinced that the murmurs shame told me were true, I made sure to go nowhere near my Bible or not even think to throw up a prayer to the only God that can save.

How could I dare draw near to God with my hands filthy from my own sin and my mind tainted with the images I had watched for far too long. No! I could not come into the presence like this—at least that's what had been taught to me by the voice of shame. "Take a few days, and this feeling will go away. Then you will be able to connect with God again." Shame would whisper in a tone that told me he was on my side. This was one of his favorites.

The more he could persuade me to run from Jesus, the more I'd let him stick around. So like a friend who listens to bad advice, I continued to ignore God and went to sleep. "Maybe when I wake up, I won't feel this ick of goo seared on my inner man," I thought as I lay down in agony. I was hurting and filled with sorrow. I felt alone and far from God. Yet despite my brokenness this is where everything changed.

In the night, when I had no control, I met the Lord in a way I hadn't before. He came in a dream to me. At the time, I had no context for the Lord speaking in dreams. I knew of a few stories in the Scriptures where men had heard from God in a dream, but this was not a reality for me. I know now that dreams are one of God's favorite ways to speak. Let me tell you the dream I had that ultimately evicted shame from the premises of my mind and heart.

I was standing at the sea of Galilee just off the shoreline in calf-deep water. I immediately noticed that my legs were buried in mud that trapped me in place. I began to try with all my might to remove myself from the mud that seemed like glue. As I pulled and pulled on my legs and attempted to remove myself, I only found myself getting more and more snug into the mud.

I began to panic. I grew exhausted and eventually began to scream for help as I gave up. I couldn't move. I was completely stuck. All of a sudden I heard the sound of someone whistling. As I looked around, I saw a man in the distance walking along the shoreline about one hundred yards away. The closer the man got, the louder and clearer the whistling. Then He was about thirty yards away.

I knew the man was whistling a melody that I had heard before. It was the bridge to "Jesus Paid It All." Here are some of the lyrics: "Jesus paid it all, all to Him I owe; [my] sin had left a crimson stain, He washed it white as snow."[5] This was the song the man was whistling, and as He got within just a few feet of me, I knew it was Jesus.

I was embarrassed to look at Him or even acknowledge Him because of where I was stuck. He came right up to me, and He was standing on top of the mud I so easily sunk into. "You look like you're stuck there; can I help you out?" Jesus joyfully chuckled my way. I nodded to Jesus in a way that gave Him permission to grab my hand. Without the slightest bit of strain where I had wiggled and wrestled with great strength, He proved that His strength was greater and hoisted me out of the mud.

As I stood there on the shore with Him, I noticed my legs, although no longer trapped in the mud, still had a layer of mud caked on them. In the dream I bent over in the shiny Galilean waters, yet even my greatest efforts failed to remove the muddy residue from my legs. "I have something for that!" Jesus boasted with excitement as He watched me in my efforts.

I realized He had a wooden bucket that had been strapped around his shoulder and rested at His side. He pulled it around, and I saw that it was filled with blood. He ripped a small piece of His garment to use as a rag, and He dipped it in the bucket of blood. Immediately, Jesus began to wipe and wash the mud off of my legs. I looked all over them, and they were completely clean and free from the goo of mud. As I was standing there unstuck and freshly cleaned, I saw

Jesus motion with His hand in a way that suggested an invitation to continue with Him down the shore. "Shall we walk?" He said with a smile.

That was the end of the dream, and I woke up. I felt the tangible presence of Jesus in a way that suggested shame was no longer camping in my room. I looked at the time on my phone, and I knew my local church was having a service within the hour. I got up, hastily got dressed, and bolted out the door to make the service. As I walked into the room, worship had already started.

Would you be able to guess what song the worship team was singing if I asked you? It was "Jesus Paid It All." I walked straight up to a leader that was not a peer in my life, and for the first time ever I confessed the sin that I wasn't currently free from. There was something about the dream that empowered me to go and invite someone that had authority over me into my process. As that leader prayed for me that day, I felt as though Jesus were washing me in His blood just like the dream. I no longer felt the goo or stain of sin lingering within me. I felt clean. I felt righteous. I felt near to God.

That was the day that Jesus broke that chain around my neck. Now, don't get me wrong—I would still fall into the sins of lust of the flesh and lust of the eyes from time to time, but here was a shift. I immediately would put on worship music, confess what I had done to people and the Lord, and fling myself into the waiting arms of Jesus. I would engage God, and I quickly found that He was eager to engage me. He had a better word than that of shame. He was a better friend with a more trusted voice.

Eventually, the identity He was giving me—the righteousness he continually spoke over me—far outweighed the invitation of the enemy to scroll, look, and linger on the synthetic drug lust was offering. I found that it actually is on *this* side of the grave that you can be free from the power of sin. The cup the Lord offers is so much better.

The problem was, I thought sin was my adversary and it was my job to slay this Goliath. Unfortunately, I was no David and no match for sin. Ten times out of ten I found sin was bigger than me, faster than me, stronger than me, and more crafty than I was. I was dominated. It wasn't until I took off the boxing gloves and raced to the feet of Jesus that I found liberation. Sin is no match for Jesus, not even in the slightest. He is the undefeated heavyweight champion that defeats the power of sin. He made a public spectacle of hell, death, and the grave. He disarmed the rulers of this world and crushed the head of the serpent with His heel. He forcefully took back the right to the hearts of the sons of men, and He deemed the unworthy holy, blameless, and above reproach.

I died to the right to fight my own battles. I found that Jesus—the very One who chuckles and laughs with you, washes you with a smile, and comes to you when you're stuck—is the same Jesus who is the Lord strong and mighty. He has never lost a battle and silences the voice of shame. He did it for me, and He'll do it for you. Take off the gloves; lean in to Jesus, and you'll see that in a single moment He can do with no effort what we tried to do with all of ours.

I often find that living an unoffendable life, possessing an unoffendable heart, truly starts with being unoffended with ourselves. What I mean is this: It's remarkably easy for us to accept that the gospel is transformative for others, especially those new to faith. Yet as we grow older in our journey with Christ, it strangely becomes easier to hold faith for these newcomers than for ourselves. We unwittingly embrace this peculiar notion that Jesus' grace and mercy wane as the years pass. We find ourselves offended by the idea that His mercies are indeed new every morning for us as well.

I have found myself frustrated with myself, thinking, "Why haven't I figured this out yet?" or "Here I am, still struggling with the same old things." But we simply cannot afford to carry this offense any longer—not toward ourselves, not toward others, and certainly not toward God.

Make It Personal

- What, if anything, have you let offense rob you of?

- What steps can you take to live with an unoffendable heart, both toward others and yourself? How might this transformation affect your relationships and your faith journey?

- Whom have you offended in your life? Write their names in a journal or on a sheet of paper that no one else will see. Ask the Lord how you can make it right and if there is anyone else who should be on your list.

- Can you recall a time when you chose to let go of an offense and trust God to handle the situation? How did this decision impact you spiritually and emotionally?

- How do you handle feelings of disappointment or offense toward yourself? Can you identify ways to cultivate self-forgiveness and embrace the idea that God's mercies are new every morning for you too?

- In challenging times, how do you nurture gratitude and joy? Can you think of a specific instance when maintaining a thankful and joyful mindset helped you overcome feelings of offense or bitterness?

Chapter 4

BETRAYAL

IF YOU DID not know, the word *salvation* appears over 160 times in the Bible, *hope* appears more than 120 times in the King James Version of the Bible, *faith* is used 247 times, and *trust* 134 times.[1] You would not argue with the fact that all these words are absolutely vital in the Christian faith. It is nearly impossible to say you're a Christian without having these words deeply embedded in your life: salvation, hope, faith, and trust.

Yet there's another word, which is also crucial, that's mentioned around 120 times in the New Testament and over 200 in the Greek Old Testament. This word, though perhaps not as exhilarating, is equally important: betray. In Greek it is *paradidōmi*,[2] and in Hebrew, betrayal, or transgression, can be considered *pešaʻ* (or *pesha*).[3] Let me pause here to delve into some biblical truths before we examine a phenomenon I have observed that has devastated many believers' faith. Conversely, I have also seen legends in the faith overcome this very challenge.

Pesha, in the Old Testament, describes a betrayal of relationships. This term is applicable to various relational breaches, such as two nations with a broken treaty or friends who break trust.[4] In contemporary terms this could be seen as brothers and sisters in the body of Christ breaking trust. Moreover, the Old Testament categorizes theft generally as robbery, but if such an act is committed by a neighbor, it is specifically termed *pesha*, indicating a deeper layer of betrayal.[5]

Betrayal—just like trust, hope, and faith—is inevitable in the life of every believer. True betrayal can only occur when it is from someone close to you. Sadly, we weren't taught this in Sunday school, and most sermons today guide us to avoid betrayal rather than teach us how to overcome it. In fact many of today's sermons on betrayal more closely resemble the talks of motivational speakers, filled with new age philosophy, rather than providing a biblical framework for overcoming betrayal.

We are often taught to leave behind toxic people and toxic thoughts to build a life of serenity and peace, as though peace is something that can be achieved through our own efforts. We forget that He is the Prince of Peace and He offers peace that surpasses all understanding.

While I am not advocating that you stay in harmful situations, what I am suggesting is that you cannot control every adverse circumstance in your life. If you try to control everything, you are likely to find yourself miserable. As believers we must learn how to die daily to the aspects of life that continue to challenge our faith.

If this is the first time you're hearing this, let it sink in: As a Christian you will face betrayal. And not just from strangers or unbelievers but from those closest to you—because true betrayal can only come from within your circle. That's what makes it so deeply hurtful. In this chapter I'll focus on a few key aspects that are paramount to seeing you make it in your faith. My friend, if you're able to die to the fear of betrayal, you will live out faith for a lifetime.

Let's start off by stating this clearly: Betrayal wasn't tucked away in the fine print when we accepted Christ. Jesus explicitly warned that the world would hate us, stating it would be brother against brother and that we would face false accusations (Matt. 10:21; 5:11). He was up front about the reality that betrayal would be a common part of our Christian journey, evidenced by whom He allowed into His inner circle. Even knowing Judas' future betrayal, Jesus kept him close, shared meals with him, and even allowed Judas the intimate act of kissing Him on the cheek toward the end of His life. I don't know about you, but to me that seems pretty contrary to what today's culture suggests.

Jesus wasn't trying to avoid betrayal; instead, He was overcoming it. Betrayal came from close friends, from the public's opinions of Him, and from religious leaders who chose to spare a notorious criminal over an innocent man. How do we come to grips with the reality that betrayal is inevitable, and how do we prevent such betrayals from jading our hearts? What do we do when betrayals cut deep and come from those closest to us? How do we respond? And how do we remain steadfast when the pain seems unbearable?

From Genesis through to the New Testament we witness numerous betrayals. From Satan's betrayal of God and Eve, to the fraternal betrayal between Cain and Abel, to Joseph and his brothers, to Saul and David, and to Judas' betrayal of Jesus, the scriptural narrative is rife with betrayal across various relationship dynamics. Betrayal knows no bounds; it respects neither position nor title. It cannot be avoided by mere holiness, as evidenced by the life of Jesus, nor can it be dispelled through diligent scripture reading, prayer, fasting, or casting out.[6]

Betrayal is like an oncoming wave in the ocean—you cannot run from it without risking being smashed by the water, nearly drowning. The only thing you can do is confront the wave directly, diving into it at the perfect angle and emerging on the other side refreshed and invigorated. I believe this chapter will achieve that for you. It will empower you to confront betrayal head-on and come out on the other side rejuvenated, full of life and breath. This chapter might unearth issues in your heart that you have not yet dealt with, but through the Holy Spirit you will emerge victorious.

We will explore betrayals in the Bible involving family and friends. I believe that by the end of this chapter, if you have experienced betrayal, your heart posture will shift. You will learn how to bless those who have betrayed you, understand what it means to truly bless your enemies, and discover the importance of maintaining a posture of humility.

Lies of Betrayal

I want to begin by exposing the lies that betrayal plants in our minds during various seasons and situations. Betrayal often attacks our minds and hearts, suggesting that the cost of following Jesus is no longer worthwhile. It can make us feel that the pain of betrayal confirms we should never follow Jesus again, or at least that we should approach Him with caution. Many people I meet, especially those my age, admit that betrayals have made them question whether their youthful zeal for Jesus was too extreme.

This couldn't be further from the truth. Here are some common lies and distorted truths that I've observed people believing after experiencing betrayal:

- Betrayal means I am living in sin.
- A true Christian cannot commit betrayal.
- If I am betrayed, it means I am not blessed.
- Betrayal forces me to forgive but never forget.
- Betrayal has made me feel foolish for trusting in God and people.
- Betrayal can simply be prayed away.
- Avoiding service to God will protect me from betrayal.
- Only leaders experience betrayal.
- Betrayal justifies my anger and any resulting sin.

Betrayal

As I prayed about this chapter, I consulted my friend Michael Koulianos, who has endured many trials but has never emerged smelling of smoke. I asked him to share his insights about overcoming betrayal for those reading this book.

Michael Koulianos

> Jesus is the ultimate pattern and our ultimate example; the Lord Himself should be our obsession, and Christ crucified defines the Christian life. Jesus was betrayed continually and often. Therefore, betrayal is part of the Christian life. While it is deeply painful, there is glory on the other side of walking through the pain with Jesus. The reality is that the crucified life is a life of pain and inexpressible joy. This combination confounds the wise and is something only God can accomplish. When those who are betrayed find deep joy in Christ Jesus, it becomes a testimony to the unbeliever and the believer. I want to encourage you to walk the road of Calvary, carrying your cross behind our Master, who carries His cross and today still bears the wounds of Calvary in His resurrected body. This is the definition of glory: pain and resurrection summed up in one person, Jesus Christ.

Trusting Again

The fear of betrayal is often scarier than betrayal itself. I remember my first trip to Six Flags when I was in high school, facing the ride called The Medusa. I was with all my cousins, eager to ride it, but the height, the twists, the turns, and the flips terrified me. Standing in line while they buzzed with excitement, I was petrified, secretly hoping the ride would break down before it was our turn. But that didn't happen.

With sweaty palms, I reached the front of the line. As the previous riders exited, the gates swung open for us to enter. I sat down, pulling the shoulder lock down as tight as I could—probably tighter than necessary because I was afraid I'd slip out. I could barely breathe. They checked everyone's seatbelts and locks, and then, with a simple "Have a good ride," the operator pressed the button.

The most terrifying sound I had ever heard began to play: click, click, click, click. The roller coaster climbed higher and higher, overlooking Santa Clarita, California. Everything below—flags, homes, people—seemed as small as grains of dirt. We reached the peak, and when the clicking stopped, I knew there was no turning back. Suddenly, with a hiss like air escaping a balloon, the coaster plunged down at what seemed to be five hundred miles per hour, racing along the tracks.

I thought, "This is the stupidest thing I've ever done." But before I knew it, we were back at the gate, the ride was over, our seatbelts were released, and we were getting off. The fear I felt before the ride was far greater than the actual experience. This, I think, is similar to how we often feel about betrayal. We spend a lifetime fearing the worst scenarios, but as we hold on to Jesus during those moments, before we know it, the ride is over and we realize we've made it through in one piece.

If you've ever been betrayed, especially as a believer (and I'm speaking right now strictly to believers), you know what I'm talking about when I mention the cost of forgetting, forgiving, and re-signing up for where God has placed you. What many overlook in the Bible is Jesus' life after the cross and before the ascension. There was a period of forty days during which He appeared to many, including the disciples. The betrayal Jesus experienced was on a whole other level, if you think about it.

He broke bread before spending the night in the Garden of Gethsemane. As His soul bore the weight of His impending crucifixion, Jesus faced a level of betrayal many of us will never understand. Can you imagine showing up to that dinner knowing the one who already sold you out was there? Jesus even declared, "Someone around this table is going to betray me" (Matt. 26:23, paraphrased). Then, after His close *friend* betrayed Him, that same individual led a group of *temple guards* to betray Jesus further. It was indeed betrayal, for Jesus said, "While I was with you daily in the temple, you did not lay hands on Me; but this hour and the power of darkness are yours" (Luke 22:53).

Then Jesus experienced betrayal from *religious leaders* who despised every aspect of His character, as His life of godliness threatened their lives of compromise. He also faced betrayal from the *elders* who supported the decision to have Him arrested and killed. Beyond this He endured the betrayal of the *crowd*—some of whom He had likely healed or prayed for—now shouting, "Barabbas, Barabbas," as they chose whom they wanted released (Luke 23:18, paraphrased). He was then betrayed by His own *government*, the Romans, who, without a fair trial or any credible evidence of a crime deserving death, sentenced Him to be crucified. And finally, He was betrayed by His own *disciples*, who fled in fear, leaving Jesus abandoned on the cross, except for the one disciple who remained (Matt. 26:56; John 19:25–26).

Jesus hung there for hours, bleeding and in excruciating pain, ultimately crying out, "My God, my God, why have you forsaken me?" (Matt. 27:46, NIV). The magnitude of the betrayal Jesus endured within those twenty-four hours likely diminishes any betrayal we might experience, making what we often call betrayal seem insignificant by comparison. He then died and was laid in a cold tomb sealed with a stone. And three days later He broke out of the grave. That is the part of the story we are all familiar with.

But what we often overlook is that in those forty days after His resurrection, Jesus modeled for us the response to betrayal. Not once do the Scriptures mention that Jesus confronted those who betrayed Him to demand an explanation. This might be uncomfortable for some, but it's important to highlight these truths from the Bible. You never see Jesus, as depicted in the Book of John, confront Peter on the shore while preparing a meal, asking, "Peter, where were you? Why did you leave me?" (See John 21:9–17.)

Nor do you find Jesus demanding a public apology from all the religious leaders and elders. You never see Jesus calling down fire from heaven upon the wicked Roman government. What blows my mind is that Jesus did not hesitate to continue His Father's business post-betrayal, unlike many of us might. He did not let the events affect His mission. Despite the pain, both internal and external—from the whips and nails to the deep wounds of betrayal—He triumphed, fully embodying both the human and divine response to such profound disloyalty.

This was only possible because He knew His purpose and understood that betrayal was an integral part of the faith. During His remaining days on earth, Jesus' testimony drew many to Him. It is said that over five hundred people saw Him (1 Cor. 15:6), and from all that Scripture reveals, Jesus did not spend those forty days grumbling, complaining, or warning others about those who betrayed Him. Instead, He focused on teaching about the kingdom of God (Acts 1:3).

We seldom help anyone by merely warning them about betrayals. Rather, we help them by showing how to walk through these trials. If anyone could have taken His foot off the gas and coasted into His ascension, it was Jesus. Yet He did not. His faith remained unshaken; He did not become bitter or angry. He did not turn into a resentful preacher using His sermons to air grievances, nor did He resort to creating sensational content to vent His frustrations. We never see Jesus publicly processing His ordeal of betrayal. By showcasing how our Savior responded to betrayal, I aim to illustrate that if we are truly Christians, then His life should be the one we are modeling our lives after.

Betrayal Bears a Mark

Just as the nails left marks of betrayal on Jesus, there are many unseen marks of betrayal that we bear. I want to clarify what it means to truly walk through betrayal as opposed to merely having a disagreement with a brother or sister. Here are three ways you can discern if you've experienced betrayal rather than a disagreement:

1. The betrayer, a person who was once close to you, intentionally broke your trust. I emphasize "intentionally" because it's crucial to differentiate between genuine betrayal and unintentional mistakes or accidents that lack malice.
2. The person acted with a willful intent to harm, undermining the trust and friendship that was once cherished.
3. Betrayal can take various forms, such as breaking trust, stealing money, or speaking ill of someone.

These criteria can help ensure we address betrayal with the seriousness it deserves, recognizing the deep wounds it can cause.

Betrayal the Teacher

Remember the first day of high school classes? You walked into the classroom, the subject was unfamiliar, the problems seemed insurmountable, and the textbook appeared to be in a foreign language. But if you had a really good teacher, by the end of the school year you would master all that you initially didn't know. And if you had a truly great teacher, the lessons learned would stick with you for decades.

Betrayal can serve as one of the greatest teachers in our lives if we view it through the right lens. It can teach us to love more deeply, to give more freely, to bless others, to recognize our own vulnerabilities where we once felt strong, and it can lead us to find Jesus in ways that flattery never will.

Remember, the Scripture says, "Woe to you when everyone speaks well of you" (Luke 6:26, NIV). Do not bite the bait of flattery, amens, agreements, and likes on your social media posts; don't conflate those things with being in right standing with God. In fact, experiencing betrayal might mean that you are in right standing with God. But how can you be sure you've truly overcome betrayal? How do you know you're not just saying you've overcome it when you're really stuffing down your offense?

Here I have listed several attributes of someone who has experienced betrayal and overcome it:

- They are meek and humble.
- They are quick to listen and slow to speak.
- They show mercy toward their betrayer, remembering Jesus' words: "Father, forgive them, for they do not know what they do" (Luke 23:34, NKJV).
- They lack any desire for revenge or retaliation.
- They do not fantasize about their betrayer's downfall.
- They do not keep a record of wrongs.

BETRAYALS IN THE BIBLE

There are a few stories in the Bible that embody true betrayal. Again, I say true betrayal because people can very easily mistake normal disputes, conflicts, and disagreements as betrayals when they are actually not. People can also minimize true betrayal as a mere dispute.

Let me show you biblically where betrayal has come into being. The obvious one, which I won't delve too deeply into, is Satan, the angel of light, betraying God by taking upon himself the desire to be God and to be worshipped. Pride within his heart fueled his betrayal. His pride and covetous desires led him to betray his Creator and lead one-third of the angels with him. His betrayal wouldn't just involve him alone; he would take many with him, ultimately damning them to hell with his decision.

Then, in Genesis we can observe the betrayal among brothers with Cain and Abel. This betrayal, unlike the one initiated by Satan, which was driven by pride, was fueled by jealousy. Cain's jealousy stemmed from his offering not pleasing the Lord, which drove him to commit murder. He picked up a rock and took the life of his brother, marking a true act of betrayal.

We also see the life of Joseph. Although his brothers were also driven by jealousy similar to Cain, their betrayal led them to abandon him in a pit and leave him for dead. The betrayal Joseph faced is distinctly different from that of Cain and Abel. Firstly, Joseph survived. We also get to follow Joseph's journey post-betrayal, which took him from the pit to Potiphar's house, then to prison, and eventually to the palace.

I'm not going to preach a sermon here about how God prepares preachers in pits for palaces, but I want to point out some obvious things that might not be so obvious. Joseph's betrayal spanned at least two decades, and he had to dwell upon it. It began with one day he spent in the pit, which was probably one of the longest days of his life because up until that point, there is no record that Joseph had ever experienced such abandonment or betrayal before. And being only seventeen years old, there were probably a lot of other emotions that he went through (Gen. 37:2, 23–24).

From the pit he wasn't pulled out and reunited with his father as he probably hoped he would be; rather, he was carried off to Potiphar's house and sold into slavery. He would spend the next thirteen years of his life both in Potiphar's house and in prison. Joseph's first betrayal was by his brothers; his second was by Potiphar's wife, and then by Potiphar himself. The wife's betrayal was that she lied and falsely accused him, and the betrayal of Potiphar was that he didn't believe Joseph, who had no telltale signs of ever being a liar.

Within such a short span of time, Joseph experienced three betrayals, and it was the third one that landed him in prison. As the years went on, like any normal person, Joseph probably revisited the memory from that moment as a seventeen-year-old boy, the day his brothers threw him in the pit. I don't think I'd be far off to say there were probably many nights where he cried many tears. There were even probably thoughts of revenge. After all, people probably have done far less to you, and you have wanted revenge at times. Imagine him.

The life of Joseph produced something that can't be overlooked. Joseph never allowed the pit and the prison to get inside his heart. He never allowed his heart to be put in a pit or a prison. He never allowed betrayal to poison his heart. One day after interpreting a dream, he found himself in the palace. The story could have ended there, and it would have given anyone who's experienced betrayal the mindset and the heart posture to say that God vindicated him and let his haters look at his success.

But Joseph's story continues, and when the famine hits, everyone is forced to come to Pharaoh. After twenty-two long years Joseph's brothers show up, and Joseph is now thirty-nine years old with the power to finally get revenge. There is no way for us to justify the actions of his brothers in this situation.

Their actions were wrong—conniving, abusive, manipulative, and downright evil. Joseph could have, at any moment, publicly shamed them, publicly killed them, or publicly exposed them, but he didn't. Instead, because he saw his brothers' remorse and repentance, with the help of the Lord he chose something that probably kept his heart pure until the day that he died—he chose mercy.

The story of Joseph is one that is encouraging and eliminates any excuses we may have for responding differently. If Joseph, who foreshadowed Jesus and did not yet have the Holy Spirit dwelling inside him (Acts 2, when the Holy Spirit descends in the Upper Room, had not yet occurred), could display mercy and compassion, then I am convinced that we, as Spirit-filled believers, have no justification for responding any differently.

It's easy for us to run circles in our minds to justify actions of retaliation due to betrayal. We can find friends that will back up our justifications; we can find books that will validate our justifications, and we could find podcasts and sermons, or social media groups. And I'm pretty sure if we were to post our betrayal online, we could easily have an angry mob that would join us and tell us how "right" we are. But remember this: You are not responsible for the things that happen to you, but you are responsible for how you respond to them.

Bless Those Who Have Betrayed You

The challenge comes when we look to bless those who have betrayed us. Blessing our enemies or those who have betrayed us is no easy task. And it is impossible to do without Jesus. We are not able to bless our enemies in our own strength.

As you've been reading, there might have been people who came to your mind throughout this chapter. There may be people whose betrayal you feel as though every day you wake up, you are having to forgive. Or maybe you're on the other end of it; maybe you've betrayed someone and you live with perpetual guilt, angry with yourself, not knowing how to receive God's forgiveness, let alone the forgiveness of others. When you fall into this trap, you're living a merciful-less Christian life, trying to work your way to salvation, which is a free gift.

It is in our human nature never to show mercy and certainly never to receive it. Our flesh will always desire an eye for an eye, a tooth for a tooth, and blood for blood. Again, I am not here to tell you what to do, only to point to the truth we see throughout the Scriptures. Betrayal is deadly to those who don't have the right perspective on it.

Over the years, I have witnessed many individuals turning away from Jesus due to the pain caused by pastors' mistakes, wrongful actions, or betrayals. I've seen people leave the faith or never even come into the faith because of believers who felt like family but ended up betraying them. I have encountered those who felt betrayed by the church and, because of situations that took place, ended up forming an entirely new theology or viewpoint of the church. See, when you view betrayal through the lens of your flesh, it has a way of becoming something that picks off the scab from an old sore so your wound will never heal. Further, betrayal through this lens is like a knife that repeatedly cuts open the wound as it tries to heal.

I have found prayer to be a powerful tool as we seek to overcome betrayal. I want you to take a step right now and pray a prayer of forgiveness. As Jesus said, "Father, forgive them, for they know not what they do" (Luke 23:24, NKJV). This might be the first time you're praying this sort of prayer or the thousandth time you're praying it.

The first prayer to follow is for those of you who have experienced betrayal firsthand. We're going to say a prayer of forgiveness and ask the Lord for your heart to be made well. In this moment, I encourage you to forgive family members, friends, fathers, mothers, siblings, aunts, uncles, grandmas, grandpas,

Betrayal

and anyone else in your life from whom you have experienced the hurt of betrayal. I encourage you to forgive neighbors, bullies, pastors, religious leaders, and more.

The second prayer we're going to pray is for those of you who admit that you have betrayed someone. I believe a couple of amazing things will happen for you as you pray this prayer: (1) You will forgive yourself and allow God's mercy to wash over you, and (2) you will likely realize that you need to ask for forgiveness from someone you betrayed, and God will give you the courage and the words to approach them. Let's pray.

Prayer 1: I've Been Betrayed

Repeat this prayer with me:

> *Father, I've been betrayed. My trust has been broken; my heart has been shattered, and my soul has been violated. I ask You that Your Holy Spirit would come and comfort me. I ask You that You would lead me to forgiveness. I pray for* (insert the name of the person or people you need to forgive), *that they would come to know You. I bless them. And I pray that You would take all ill feelings away from my heart. Give me Your eyes to see them how You see them. May I never curse them in my heart or with my words. Just as Joseph forgave his brothers, just as Jesus forgave those who put Him on the cross, may I forgive those who betrayed me. In Jesus' name, amen.*

You may need to pray the previous prayer more than once. Some may feel a release in their hearts immediately; for others it may take some time. Be patient and be persistent in your forgiveness.

Prayer 2: I've Betrayed Someone

Repeat this prayer with me:

> *Father, I've betrayed* (insert the name of the person or people you betrayed). *I ask You that You would forgive me. I ask You that You would wash my mind and my heart of the offense I've caused and the sin that's been done. Forgive me for not modeling the life that You modeled. Let me receive Your mercy and forgiveness. Speak to me of the areas I need to make right with You and with man. If there are ways I can repay things that I've taken, may I do so with a joyful heart. Just as the man in the New Testament who met Jesus paid back double everything he stole, help me restore anything that was taken. And may I never walk in betrayal again. In Jesus' name, amen.*

Again, you may need to pray this more than once. Some may feel a release in their hearts immediately; for others, it may take some time. Be patient and persistent in your prayer, and allow God to speak to you if there are any ways you can make things right.

I would like to add this disclaimer: Forgiving your betrayer has everything to do with you and your heart. There is no pressure or need for the relationship to return to how it was before the betrayal, nor would I ever suggest someone return to an abusive situation. I encourage you to focus on your own healing so your soul can be whole and well.

Make It Personal

- In what ways can betrayal, particularly from those close to you, be a test of your faith? How have you navigated such experiences in your own life?

- In what ways can you see betrayal as a potential teacher in your spiritual journey? How can this perspective affect the way you react to those who have wronged you?
- What are some lies or distorted truths that betrayal has led you to believe about yourself or your faith? How can you confront these misconceptions with biblical truth?
- How can you cultivate a heart posture of mercy and forgiveness toward those who betray you?
- Ask the Lord to highlight to you anyone you need to forgive. What steps can you take to forgive those who have betrayed you and to release any lingering bitterness or resentment, allowing for healing and reconciliation?
- Have you betrayed anyone? Ask the Lord if there is someone you need to ask forgiveness of.

Chapter 5

BITTERNESS

BITTERNESS AND UNFORGIVENESS, though similar, are very different at their core. The root of bitterness produces a different fruit than the root of unforgiveness. The trap of bitterness I see plagues so many, especially Christians. And Christians young and old have become so entangled in the root of bitterness that we no longer look like Christ. Before we get into the depths of what bitterness is, I want to share a quote: "The worst thing in life is not to die but to live with bitterness."[1] When I read this quote and really started thinking about it, I thought, "This is partially true. But bitterness is indeed more closely akin to death because when we are in its snare, we are not able to live in the fullness that God has for us." Bitterness has the power to hold you in a silent prison while at the same time blinding you as its prey.

I was hesitant to include a chapter on bitterness in my book, but as I pondered aspects of the flesh that legends in the faith have to die to, I could not escape this as an important one to discuss. After all, Jesus spoke about the dangers of bitterness and emphasized that it should not take root in our hearts. He knew the threat of what would happen to our entire lives if the root of bitterness dwelled in us.

I've always wondered about that verse in Matthew 24:12 that talks about "the love of many [growing] cold" (NKJV). It's hard to understand how close friends and people I've run with in ministry can end up divided, or how the body of Christ can experience church and ministry splits, leading to years of disunity and accusations among believers. But as I've watched events unfold over the last decade, I can see how bitterness plays a key role in causing our love to grow cold.

Bitterness is like quicksand—it slowly takes you and your heart captive and doesn't let go; it suffocates you the more you struggle to escape it. And ministry bitterness seems to be worse because we often feel as though since we're Christians, the things we go through shouldn't be happening to us, right? I have found bitterness to be a major contributor to why many Christians become stuck and unable to move forward in their lives. There seems to be a moment, a person, or a situation that occurred that many individuals just can't move past. That's when bitterness comes crashing in, betraying them and telling them they're the victim, which only drives them deeper into the sinking sand of their pain.

The central focus of this chapter is inspired by a verse you've probably read many times before: "See to it that no one comes short of the grace of God; that no root of bitterness springing up causes trouble, and by it many be defiled" (Heb. 12:15). When we look at this verse, there are a few things that the writer is warning us about. The first warning is this: "See to it that no one comes short of the grace of God" (Heb. 12:15). *Coming short* of the grace of God here is the Greek word *hystereō*, which simply means "to be inferior," to "be destitute," to "lack," or to "suffer need."[2]

We can see that when we get into a state of mind where the grace of God is not enough for us, or where we lack understanding of God's grace for us, that quickly turns into us lacking the grace of God for our brothers and sisters. Our lack of God's grace is where we can see the root of bitterness springing up in our hearts, causing us trouble and ultimately leading to our defilement, or *miainō* in Greek. *Miainō* means "defiled," contaminated, soiled, and polluted.[3]

I'm about to delve into some deep matters of the heart, but first I want to highlight the severity and depth of the words we read in our English Bibles when considered in their original language. See, the author of Hebrews is not lightly suggesting that we merely lack grace for ourselves, nor is the root of bitterness something we should tolerate in our lives. Understand that what you tolerate will eventually dominate, and bitterness genuinely contaminates, soils, and pollutes our faith. It is not something you can allow to dwell in your temple.

Just as you would never allow a thief or a criminal within your physical home—where your family, young siblings, spouse, or children reside—you should not allow bitterness to inhabit your personal temple, the dwelling place of the Holy Spirit. And just as you would do everything possible to remove a criminal from your home to protect your loved ones and belongings, I pray this chapter will help you adopt this mindset if you are grappling with bitterness: that by any means necessary, you get it out of your life through the Word of God and the Holy Spirit.

The word *bitterness* itself is quite intriguing. Often when we hear it, we immediately think of people or situations where we've seen it demonstrated. Yet this leads us to assign various degrees or severities to what we consider bitterness, which may vary greatly between individuals. I might see it as severe, and you might not see it as severe. Before we delve into how bitterness affects our hearts, lives, and faiths, let's examine its original meaning in the Greek to understand the gravity and implications of harboring such feelings.

Pikría is the Greek word used for bitterness, and its meaning might surprise you. This term was used to describe plants that were inedible or bore poisonous fruits.[4] If you understand how roots work, you know that every root will inevitably produce fruit, as noted in Hebrews 12:15. Therefore if the fruit of bitterness is poisonous, it is dangerous not only to us but also to those who partake in our lives. The Greeks also described bitterness as long-standing resentment or as a spirit unwilling to reconcile.[5] Now that you grasp the severity of this concept, let's explore more scriptures that clearly outline the dangers and effects of bitterness. You might debate the extent of bitterness's impact, but ultimately, all our opinions must defer to the authority of God's Word.

- Proverbs 17:25: "A foolish son brings grief to his father and bitterness to the mother who bore him" (NIV).
- Ephesians 4:31–32: "Get rid of all bitterness, rage and anger, brawling and slander, along with every form of malice. Be kind and compassionate to one another, forgiving each other, just as in Christ God forgave you" (NIV).
- Romans 12:19: "Do not take revenge, my dear friends, but leave room for God's wrath, for it is written: 'It is mine to avenge; I will repay,' says the Lord" (NIV).
- Proverbs 14:10: "Each heart knows its own bitterness, and no one else can share its joy" (NIV).
- James 3:14: "But if you harbor bitter envy and selfish ambition in your hearts, do not boast about it or deny the truth" (NIV).

From the Old Testament to the New, it's clear that bitterness is not something we want in our lives. But sadly it often creeps in unnoticed, gradually gaining a foothold through various situations or the influence of others. Bitterness takes root in areas of our lives that we have not fully surrendered to the Holy Spirit. It's evident that bitterness never leads to godliness. Let's take a moment to examine some of the effects that bitterness can have in our lives.

Fruits of Bitterness

Now, there are signs that clearly indicate if the root of bitterness has sprouted in your heart. These symptoms remain consistent, whether the root is deep or shallow. Here, I will outline both practical and spiritual indicators that you may be harboring bitterness. Remember, no heart is too hardened or root too entrenched for God to heal. While there may be additional signs, these are the ones I've observed most frequently over my decade of following Jesus and working with people:

- Bitterness leads to *sleepless nights*, as bitterness will literally eat away at you, not giving you rest.

- *Fatigue* throughout your day is another sign of bitterness. Because you have no rest, you have no strength. You may think this is due to working too hard or doing too much, but if you were to add up your day and the hours you worked, they would not equate to the exhaustion you feel. This is how you know you have the root of bitterness.

- A *negative personality* goes hand in hand with bitterness, as bitterness can never celebrate anything; it can only remain miserable.

- *Low self-esteem* and low confidence in God are also sacrifices on the altar of bitterness.

- Bitterness will *not let you keep relationships long* because it doesn't allow you to trust. Bitterness keeps you suspicious of people and their motives even if those people are credible and godly.

- Bitterness will leave you *disappointed* in everything and everyone. It robs you of any expectation, and then when things don't happen, it says, "See, I told you so," or, "I knew nothing good would ever come," or, "I knew I couldn't trust anybody."

- Bitterness will cause *irritability* and rob you of joy.
- *Sarcasm* is the language of bitterness.
- Bitterness *attracts other bitter people.* You could be in a room with a thousand Christians, and if you're a bitter person, you will find the other bitter people. It's almost like the way flies are attracted to garbage. If you put garbage outside, you'll notice that all the flies will huddle around the same area. So too bitter people huddle around bitterness.
- A bitter person will see how a group of people *didn't meet their needs* and not consider all the good those people have done.
- A bitter person loves to *talk about their wounds* and the wounds of others but has no interest in seeing those wounds healed.
- A bitter person will always paint themselves as the *safe place to process* hurt, or say you're a safe place to process, even though this is the thousandth time they have processed the same issue. They do not want to get rid of bitterness; they just want to waste your time.
- A bitter person will take one verse *out of context* that they feel justifies their bitterness, while neglecting the many scriptures about unity and restoration.

- A bitter person always has a good excuse as to why they should *not go to church* or be connected to a godly community, as bitterness leads to a *lone-ranger mindset*.

- A bitter person will always *clump groups of people together*, and you'll hear them say things like, "Well, the church is all fake," or, "Everyone in the church is the same."

- Bitter people *process their gossip* in prayer meetings in the name of praying for the person.

- Bitterness will always *make you feel unappreciated* and that your life is never seen, you're never heard, and you're never understood, as bitterness always seeks to be seen, heard, and understood.

- Bitter people *feel they have been hurt, misused, and abused* in any situation they didn't feel recognized in.

- One of the last fruits of bitterness that I want to expound on a little bit more is that of *gossip*.

This list is designed to help you recognize and address the root of bitterness before it overtakes your spiritual and personal life.

Bitterness and Gossip

Bitterness and gossip often go hand in hand, as gossip fuels the growth and spread of bitterness. Often bitterness cannot survive without gossip—it's like oxygen to a fire. Believe it or not, one effective way to stop bitterness in the life of a believer is to cut off the gossip and instead talk with the Lord, seeking His heart for individuals rather than trying to get others to agree with you. Gossip is one of the most dangerous elements in the body of Christ, within communities, churches, friendships, and the heart of a Christian. Ephesians 4:31 instructs us, "Let all *bitterness* and *wrath* and *anger* and *clamor* and *slander* [gossip] be put away from you, along with all *malice*" (emphasis added).

Because of social media, I have seen gossip become more prevalent in today's generation. It takes many shapes and forms and is often justified. The Bible warns us in Proverbs 20:19 not to associate with one who is given to gossip. Additionally, Proverbs 16:28 states that gossip separates close friends. Gossip is a tool used by bitterness to divide and conquer. Countless friendships that God intended to flourish have been destroyed by bitterness and gossip.

The heart of gossip is never a good one. The heart of gossip is never to cover another but only to expose them. It never heals; it humiliates. It is never humble; it is always haughty. It does not desire reconciliation but furthers division. I'll conclude with this: Sadly, gossip has become the modern-day believer's entertainment. We are no longer captivated by what God says about people, but instead, we fascinate ourselves with what others say about them. Rather than seeking the next headline from a news article about a church or an individual, delve into the headlines of your Bible and read the Scriptures. No good can ever come from gossip. Cut the oxygen off, and the flame of bitterness will slowly begin to die.

How Bitterness Affects Our Hearts

Our hearts, as described in Scripture, represent our thoughts and emotions. As stated in 1 John 3:20, even when our hearts condemn us, "God is greater than our hearts" (NIV). The term *hearts* isn't just a simplistic depiction; it signifies a complex mix of our emotional and decision-making faculties. For example, you may harbor a negative thought against someone and momentarily desire revenge. Yet when the compassionate part of your emotions engages, the outcome shifts away from revenge. This dynamic showcases the profound influence of our hearts.

The Bible emphasizes the importance of the heart in Romans 10:9–10: If we believe in our hearts, we shall be saved. Clearly, our hearts hold significant value to God. Our hearts are akin to soil; the seeds we plant within them will take root and bear fruit. I've witnessed how bitterness can turn the most beautiful of hearts into vessels of pain, envy, and mistrust. I've seen bitterness steal the innocence out of young believers because they were not taught how to die to bitterness and put it on the cross.

See, bitterness is encompassed in that Bible verse urging us to pick up our cross and deny ourselves—it's captured in the word *ourselves*. (See Matthew 16:24.) I remember one of the first times I met Todd White (whom we'll hear from in chapter 10). We were hanging out, discussing various situations. Honestly, I was amazed, not because of the healings—I had seen plenty of those—or even his powerful sermons but because of the consistency of his life regardless of the outcomes. I had never met a believer like him, whose faith was so steadfast.

I was often taught that there were situations that justified feeling certain ways, that bitterness was inevitable and happens to the best of us. However, getting to know Todd, I witnessed the various challenges he faced. One Sunday I arrived at his church to find picketers outside, branding him a false prophet. I thought, "Wow, what a way to enter church." Astonished by the hostility as I entered, I initially thought it was their first appearance. However, Todd informed me that they had been coming faithfully every Sunday for years. He even mentioned, half jokingly, that he hoped they would meet Jesus too.

I marveled at how Todd remained unaffected by bitterness. People claiming to be Christians had taken the time to come to his church and stand outside just to slander and accuse him, yet he harbored no resentment toward them. You've probably heard the saying that it's not the water outside but the water that gets inside the ship that causes it to sink. Similarly, while bitterness shown against you might prompt compassion within you if you handle it in a godly way, the moment it infiltrates your heart, it starts to corrode all the goodness inside you and alters your perception of others, turning brothers and sisters into perceived enemies. Once again, bitterness leads you to a place you never wanted to go, and it takes more than you wanted to give.

The story I'm about to share is one that brings me to tears every time I hear it. Nothing can truly prepare a parent for the death of their child. This is a story from a friend who is a pastor and chose to remain anonymous. His experience powerfully shows how the darkest situations can arise, but bitterness does not have to be the outcome.

Anonymous Pastor

My wife and I got married not so young but full of hope. We had led a Christian life serving in the congregation, we had finished our degrees, and our marriage was growing every day.

Thank God our first child was born a year and a half after we got married, and then we got pregnant again. Everything was going very well until our eldest son presented symptoms that seemed strange to us and worried us. We took him to the doctor, and after several tests he was diagnosed with a blood disease that was terminal.

For us it was a shock to be going through something

like this, as we had never expected that we would walk through such a hard season. After three and a half years of watching my son battle his illness, endure very painful treatments, and spend long weeks in the hospital, we watched our precious son pass away.

The pain that my wife and I walked through was too much to bear. By the grace of God and God alone, He helped my heart and gave me strength to be able to walk through this trying season with my wife. On top of all that we were going through, my wife had entered into a deep depression. Her desire to live had died with our son, and she no longer wanted to do the things she once did, like eat, go to church, and take care of our other son, who was still very young.

I remember when she told me that it was as if her chest was open and bleeding nonstop. The pain was emotional; it was unbearable. Unfortunately, the local church we were going to had no idea how to navigate such a thing, which only amplified our pain and even the temptation to be bitter.

Finally, one day my wife told me: "You can continue serving God. I've come this far; I don't plan to return to church, and I don't want to serve God either. I can't believe God allowed something like that. I'm done." When I heard those words, it was so painful for me. The pain from our son's passing was too much, and now this seemed to be even worse. Not long after, while still depressed, she got pregnant again, and we hoped this would take her out of depression. But it didn't; she continued with a depression that didn't seem to end.

Every day that went by, my wife would not leave her room, sometimes spending days in her bed. I was forced to take care of my youngest son, work, and keep the house afloat. I cried out to the Lord and said: "What can I do, Lord? It seems like everything is sinking." Imagine being a husband, a father, in this situation—not understanding what God is doing yet choosing Him. Once after praying, I heard the Lord say, "Your wife doesn't want Me in her life. But I love her, and from now on, I will love her through you."

Every day, and by the grace of God, I was able to bring her breakfast in bed and show her the love of Jesus without words. Day after day it was a struggle, but little by little the ice that was in her heart melted, and she returned to the Lord. Nothing has been easy, but I can assure you that God has worked in a wonderful way.

What impacted me the most about this story was that bitterness never took root throughout this entire season. Although this pastor had every reason to be bitter with God, he chose to trust Him even in the midst of their deepest pain.

Bitterness Affects Our Lives and Destroys Our Faith

So often bitterness profoundly impacts our lives and relationships, sometimes leading us to part ways with others. It's likely you've encountered a pastor or leader—and if not yet, you probably will—who has fallen prey to the effects of bitterness. This is often evident in their sermons, which may reveal underlying insecurities. Although names are not mentioned, the slight slander makes it clear whom they are referencing. You might have also met other believers striving to build something for God, yet bitterness underpins their foundation. No matter how much they try, nothing they build can be pure until the bitterness is eradicated.

Unlike a motivational speaker whose goal is to build you up for a better life, the enemy uses bitterness in our lives to destroy us and, more significantly, to shipwreck your faith. Bitterness often leads to sin, and as the Bible teaches, "The wages of sin is death" (Rom. 6:23). That means that if you work for sin, your paycheck is death. Many Christians who fall into sin have bitterness lurking nearby. As bitterness isolates them—keeping them from the Word of God through pride or shame—it convinces them that they are justified, elevating their source of truth above the Word of God. It's reminiscent of old cartoons where a villain lays a breadcrumb trail to trap someone; as the victim follows, eating one breadcrumb after another, they head toward destruction. So too does bitterness lead to ruin.

Bitterness infiltrates even the lives of good and godly men in the Bible, as no one is immune to its effects. Consider Job, a man of character and wealth as initially described in the Book of Job. Satan, described as a coward, has to ask God's permission to test Job, highlighting that even he is subject to God's authority. He receives permission after God boasts of Job's faithfulness. Subsequently, Job loses all his sheep and servants to a heavenly fire. Job's response? Worship. (See Job 1:1–3, 6–12, 16, 20.)

All this unfolds in chapter 1. Then, in chapter 2 Satan again requests God's permission to afflict Job, this time targeting his health (Job 2:4–6). When permission is granted, it greatly offends Job's wife, who even tells him to "curse God and die" (Job 2:9). It's important to note that before this, Job's wife had never cursed God. But as their livelihood and Job's health are compromised, bitterness overtakes her, pushing her to the point of cursing God. Yet at this juncture, Job only curses the day he was born, not the Lord. (See Job 2:1–6, 9–10; 3:1–3.)

As the narrative progresses, Job's friends enter the scene. The first offers poor advice. By Job chapter 6 more misguided counsel had come from other friends. (See Job 4–5.) It is not until this moment that Job speaks and eventually declares, "Therefore I will not restrain my mouth; I will speak in the anguish of my spirit, I will complain in the bitterness of my soul" (Job 7:11). Clearly, Job's heart is burdened. His life continues to experience many ups and downs in the ensuing chapters.

Finally, in chapter 38 God responds:

- "Then the LORD answered Job from the whirlwind and said, 'Who is this who darkens the divine plan by words without knowledge?'" (Job 38:1–2, NASB).

- "Where were you when I laid the foundation of the earth? Tell Me, if you have understanding" (Job 38:4).

- "Have you ever in your life commanded the morning, and made the dawn know its place?" (Job 38:12, NASB).

- "Have you understood the expanse of the earth? Tell Me, if you know all of this" (Job 38:18).

- "Can you raise your voice to the clouds, so that an abundance of water will cover you?" (Job 38:34, NASB).

Why am I saying all this? Because Job's journey of pain, the bad advice from his friends, and the loss of everything leads to some bitterness in his heart. And when he begins to question God, God begins to show him how vast He was. Job's heart begins to align, not understanding why things happened or why they occurred as they did but knowing he couldn't let bitterness remain in his heart. Job responds to the Lord, "Behold, I am insignificant; what can I say in response to You? I put my hand on my mouth" (Job 40:4, NASB). Instead of remaining in bitterness, Job's heart turns to God, and a few chapters later he continues, "I know that You can do all things....Therefore I have declared that which I did not understand, things too wonderful for me, which I do not know....Therefore I retract, and I repent, sitting on dust and ashes" (Job 42:2–3, 6, NASB). Shortly thereafter the Bible says the Lord restored Job's fortunes; he prayed for his friends, and the Lord increased all that he had twofold (Job 42:10).

Job's story is one of the most beautiful illustrations of a man who, although he was blessed, lost everything, battled poor advice, endured physical trials and tribulations, lost loved ones, questioned God, and even cursed the day he was born. It seems everything was setting him up to remain bitter forever, yet at the mention of repentance God blesses Job with twice as much as before. The lesson here is profound: Even if you have been bitter, there are steps to walk out of bitterness, with repentance as the foremost step.

In Job's life we see that nothing excuses bitterness to dwell within a believer—not the loss of a job or a marriage, not the passing of a loved one, or a fallout with a ministry. While it's true that experiencing these hardships is painful, we are not accountable for what happens to us. But we are responsible for how we respond.

Overcome Bitterness: Cling to God's Promises

Now that we understand the fruits of bitterness, how dangerous its root is, how to identify it, and why we absolutely don't want it (I hope you feel this way after all you've read), it's time to serve bitterness an eviction notice and expel it from our temple. Bitterness cannot simply be prayed away; it often accompanies self-righteousness. When I say that only the revelation of the cross can help you nail it to the cross, I mean you need to recall the price that was paid for you and allow your heart to release the pain of your past.

Though it may seem that bitterness, often feeling justified, is the hardest thing to die to, the way out is through the cross. It's easy to believe that Jesus can set a drug addict free, but somehow it's harder to believe He can free you from bitterness. We might find it easier to have faith that He can save a prostitute, but we struggle to believe He can uproot the effects of bitterness. We would even say we have faith that God could save a prodigal, but when it comes to our bitterness, His arm is too short to reach us.

But the good news is that the Word of God tells a different story. The Bible is filled with promises to believers that go far beyond material gains such as new cars, debt relief, random checks in the mail, and a fancy jet. I'm talking about promises that are eternal. Did you know the Bible contains 7,487 promises from God to man, 991 from one man to another, 2 from God the Father to His Son, and 290 from man to God—over 8,000 in total?[6] We obviously can't explore each one here, but as 2 Corinthians 1:20 assures us, all God's promises are *yes* and *amen*. Here are just a few of God's promises for you to reflect on:

- **His promise of not leaving us:** God will never leave or forsake us (Heb. 13:5), providing constant support during times of bitterness.

- **His promise of peace:** He gives peace that surpasses all understanding (Phil. 4:7), and it is greater than the lies of bitterness.

- **His promise of support in struggles:** His instruction to cast our cares upon Him reveals that He wants to sustain us through both our moments of success and our mess (1 Pet. 5:7).

- **His promise of forgiveness:** Confessing our sins leads to immediate forgiveness (1 John 1:9), offering a path out of bitterness.

- **His promise of escape from temptation:** God promises a way out of every temptation (1 Cor. 10:13), affirming that bitterness does not define us.

- **His promise of answering:** God demonstrates that He cares about our needs by assuring us that He will meet our asking, seeking, and knocking (Matt. 7:7).

- **His promise of wisdom:** God assures us that wisdom will be given when we ask for it (Jas. 1:5).

- **His promise of renewed strength:** The promise of renewed strength if we persist in faith enables us to endure without exhaustion (Isa. 40:31).

- **His promise of keeping His word:** God's steadfastness assures us that even when we fail, His promises remain secure (Num. 23:19).

We can't merely be believers who uphold His laws; we must also cherish His promises. These promises empower us to live lives of freedom and to conquer bitterness.

Make It Personal

- Have you ever experienced any of the fruit of bitterness discussed in this chapter? How did bitterness affect the way you serve the Lord and others?

- How do you distinguish between bitterness and unforgiveness in your own life? What specific signs or feelings help you identify them?

- How do you think bitterness can impact a person's relationship with God and their ability to live out their faith authentically?

- How do you manage negative thoughts and emotions before they turn into bitterness? What spiritual practices help you maintain a healthy heart?

- Which promises of God resonate with you the most in helping to combat bitterness? How can you incorporate these promises into your daily life?

- Reflect on a time when you successfully overcame bitterness. What lessons did you learn, and how did it transform your life and faith journey?

Chapter 6

UNFORGIVENESS

"I WILL NEVER FORGIVE you. You've hurt me beyond forgiveness. You've taken from me, and now I'm going to take from you. I may forgive you, but I will never forget what you've done to me." These words were all too common in my childhood home. How could a family, divided by divorce, brokenness, and hardships, know anything else?

Unforgiveness became my shield against further pain. Throughout my childhood I was consistently disappointed by those closest to me. As you've read the previous chapters, you likely anticipated that unforgiveness would be a topic we'd address. To be a legend in the faith, one cannot harbor unforgiveness. As we've learned throughout this book, to be a legend in the faith requires laying your life down. Unforgiveness, by contrast, keeps the focus squarely on oneself rather than on this essential surrender of self. Unforgiveness acts like cancer within the body of a believer—it kills slowly and subtly. It loves to lurk behind the unaddressed hurts and pains, waiting like a thief in the night to steal one of the greatest revelations ever bestowed upon mankind: being forgiven. When you harbor unforgiveness, truly understanding the forgiveness that God extends to you becomes impossible.

There are not many things that Jesus said the lost could use to identify us as His followers, but He did tell us that the world will recognize us by how we love one another (John 13:35). My prayer for this chapter is that it helps you understand what biblical forgiveness truly is—that you would first receive it from the Lord and then extend it to others. This chapter includes stories of individuals who have faced real problems, intense pain, and injustices, yet have chosen to forgive. I will break down what forgiveness is and what it is not, and I'll explain how sometimes forgiveness in the heart may lead to reconciliation and restoration but not necessarily to resuming a full relationship.

Forgiveness is a gift that came at a high price—not purchased with dollars, diamonds, silver, or gold, but purchased with the blood of the Son of God, Jesus, who hung on the cross. The purpose of this forgiveness is to restore our right standing with God and to renew our union and communion with Him, as it was before sin messed it up.

Jesus emphasized the importance of Christians releasing unforgiveness throughout the Word. Forgiveness is as essential to the Christian faith as air is to breathing. As Christians it is critical that we relinquish any unforgiveness in our hearts, for forgiveness is one of the primary defining marks setting us apart from the world. I would argue that forgiveness is the greatest miracle in human history. In my view it is a far more significant sign and wonder than the healing of a deaf ear or a blind eye. It surpasses even the miraculous growth of a leg or the discovery of gold dust in a church meeting. To me forgiveness far outweighs any physical manifestation or experience, including those where we jump, shake, and clap.

Forgiveness is both a physical and a spiritual encounter. It has the power to literally set free the person you harbor unforgiveness toward while simultaneously setting free your own heart. Forgiveness is even more impactful than raising your hands in a church service, shouting "Amen!" to a preacher, or faithfully tithing every week. None of these acts carry weight if you are not walking in forgiveness. You could be the most polished preacher with the most eloquent words, yet still choosing to walk in unforgiveness would be profoundly hypocritical. As a brother in the faith, I urge you to stay vigilant so that together we can remain strong in the Lord, choosing daily to release any unforgiveness in our hearts, and lay down our lives for Jesus. If you are hanging on to a lifestyle of unforgiveness, be aware of how loudly that speaks to those in your life—louder than any message you preach about forgiveness. While it's easy to fool those around us into believing we have forgiven, we cannot fool God.

This chapter became near and dear to my heart as I was writing it, as I too am not above being hurt and wounded. I have often said to many younger guys I've poured into that I too have been hurt and had opportunities for offense but that they would never know who hurt me or what those people did because the moment I forgave them, I let it go. I won't go into great detail about the things I walked through, but I will say that like other people, I have had to bring my offenses to the cross and I've had to understand that all people are broken, whether those people are my family, my friends, or even people I went to church with. In the same way that I have needed forgiveness, I have forgiven them. There were even instances when I would sense unforgiveness within myself and I would bless that individual in some way or fashion. I would bless them because I knew that where my treasure was, so would my heart lie. I never desired to hold bitterness in my heart, but I desired that I would always remain in a posture of forgiveness and mercy.

But what is forgiveness, really? What does it look like? How is it practiced? Are there specific sins God forgives and others He judges? Does forgiveness mean letting people off the hook for their actions? Is forgiveness absolutely necessary for one to be a Christian? And if I forgive, does that make me a pushover?

As a millennial, I witnessed the rise of the "celebrity Christian" era in America. This period was characterized by cool sneakers, appealing Instagram posts, nice cars, and photos with other "famous" preachers—elements that heavily influenced my generation. Not only were these traits modeled, but they also became the aspirational goals for many young preachers. The glamorous life of frequent travel and preaching suggested success; the more followers one had on social media, the more authoritative they appeared. Leaders and pastors who mingled with celebrities were often perceived as having God's special favor.

I think we absorbed, without explicit teaching, that fame was synonymous with God's favor. Fame was emphasized even more than faithfulness. We seldom considered whether the attributes of a true Christian were being modeled in those who were following such platforms. In the Western church, at least, we were enamored by the external, equating the external mark of success with spiritual achievement and often neglecting foundational teachings such as forgiveness. I'm not aiming to point fingers or claim this was intentional on anyone's part; this is simply the church culture I experienced growing up. Rarely did I ever see what it looked like to navigate real-life problems with people, and foundational aspects of faith were rarely discussed in public or social forums.

Over the years, unresolved unforgiveness has escalated into feuds among brothers and sisters in the faith and among different denominations and ministries. I have witnessed books written by one denomination against another and conferences where groups of Christians criticize one another. I even dare to mention documentaries produced under the guise of exposing heresy, while what is often labeled as "exposure" merely reflects differences within the body—some are hands and some are feet, yet how can the hand say to the foot, "I have no need of you"? (1 Cor. 12:21, ESV).

For years, even decades, the global church has struggled to live out the teaching of Mark 11:25, where Jesus says, "And when you stand praying, if you hold anything against anyone, forgive them, so that your Father in heaven may forgive you your sins" (NIV). Additionally, Matthew 6:14 states, "For if you forgive other people when they sin against you, your heavenly

Father will also forgive you" (NIV). I once heard someone claim this verse could not be taken literally, but I contend that it must be. How can you truly receive forgiveness if you do not understand it? Understanding that you are forgiven compels you to forgive others.

Forgiveness was what initially drew many of us to the cross. So how did our church culture stray so far from it? When did we start believing that some people deserve forgiveness and others do not? When did cancel culture become more influential than the culture of the cross? What are the perils of choosing not to forgive, and in what situations are we called to forgive? When did we develop a culture where we forgive the offender but not the offended, or vice versa?

The story I'm about to share comes from another friend who prefers to remain anonymous. Her life unexpectedly spiraled into turmoil, placing her in circumstances she could never have imagined. Despite numerous opportunities for unforgiveness to take root, choosing forgiveness has ushered her into a life of freedom in God. It's important to note that everyone's story differs, and the accounts you'll read below are meant to inspire, not serve as exact blueprints, because each situation is unique. My hope is that these stories, alongside Scripture, will inspire you not to let unforgiveness extinguish your faith or disrupt your walk with God.

Anonymous Young Mom

I was a fifteen-year-old girl who found herself pregnant. Terrified and full of shame, my options seemed very limited. About a year later, at the age of sixteen, I found myself with a newborn son whom I adored beyond life itself. I lived in a very physically, mentally, and emotionally abusive relationship with the father of my son. At seventeen I found myself being married to this person without anyone ever knowing what I was enduring. I lived this way for the next ten years. In this time we had our second son. I thought maybe at some point he would change.

I grew up in church and met my husband in church. He was part of the worship team. I never understood how someone on the worship team could play music for God and then go home and be abusive toward me. When I finally decided to leave my husband, I had to leave the church I grew up in, never leaving God, though.

Ultimately when leaving the church, you drift away from God. Please know I never blamed God for anything I went through. Our church talked about me and hated me, never knowing what I endured with this man. To only be judged in their eyes, I was the worst person.

When I finally left and told my family what was going on, it was very hard for my own mother to believe me because if you had ever met my ex-husband, you wouldn't believe what I was telling you either. He portrayed himself to be this perfect guy who would never raise his voice. My mother, knowing the church we attended for so many years, advised me to let our old church know why I left so they wouldn't judge me. I decided that the One who knows why I left is my God. I never told anyone.

I was very hurt, and I hated my ex-husband and the church for many years. Not only did I endure this abuse for many years from my ex-husband, but he ultimately took my kids and moved without telling me. For the next five years I couldn't find my sons, which caused my anger to grow toward him. In my heart I didn't want to go to church because people always judge. I couldn't understand how people who go to church live like that. I stayed away for many years. I had many failed relationships. Between all this I had three more children.

Finally, I met my husband whom I'm married to today. We went through our own demons from our past. My husband loves God, and that was the biggest difference. We both love God and each other. With many years of counseling and going to church, we still had our ups and downs, but we never lost hope in God. Looking back I can truly say from the bottom of my heart that I have forgiven my ex-husband and prayed for his soul to be saved.

When we judge people who have gone through a crisis or are being judged, we don't know the hurt we are adding to people's lives. Instead, get on your knees and pray for them. I have learned to love and forgive the people we would say are unforgivable and should never be forgiven. God has forgiven me for all my sins, and I couldn't ever repay Him for that. So I choose to love and forgive.

Reflecting on this story, there are many angles and insights to consider. I want to focus on a few key aspects. Physical abuse, as described, should never occur, and the pain experienced by this individual was substantial. In discussing this with her, it was evident that legal action could have been justified against the perpetrator. However, the choice made by this person was to forgive. She shared a powerful insight with me, stating, "This individual's life and what they've had to go through living with themselves is a punishment of its own."

It's common for us to quickly form opinions on how we would handle similar situations, reminiscent of football fans shouting at their television screens. They critique the game with snack-stained fingers, clad in team jerseys they've bought but not earned, comfortably detached from the actual challenges of the sport. It's somewhat amusing, isn't it? It is safe to say that each person is unique, and our responses to situations should be guided by biblical principles, as interpreted through the lens of Scripture and directed by the Holy Spirit.

How Important Is Forgiveness?

Before diving into the practical aspects that follow, I want to walk you through a few key verses from the Book of Matthew in chapter 18. After addressing His disciples' questions about who would be the greatest, Jesus discusses stumbling blocks, and He advises, "If your eye causes you to stumble, pluck it out" (Matt. 18:4–9). He then shares the parable of leaving the ninety-nine sheep to find the one, and He discusses the process of restoring a brother who falls (Matt. 18:12–17). The chapter crescendos with teachings on forgiveness.

Don't be discouraged if you find forgiveness challenging. Peter likely felt the same, as his question to Jesus seems not just general but deeply personal. In Matthew 18:21 Peter asks, "Lord, how many times shall my brother sin against me and I still forgive him?" He suggests, "Up to seven times?" as a seemingly generous limit (Matt. 18:21, NASB).

Can you already tell that this question was one that Peter wasn't really looking for Jesus to answer? It appears he believed he already had the answer. Peter might have thought offering forgiveness seven times was quite generous—after all, forgiving a brother repeatedly seemed adequately merciful. Yet Jesus extended this concept far beyond Peter's suggestion, saying, "I do not say to you, up to seven times, but up to seventy times seven" (Matt. 18:22). Quick math here—that's 490 times. I don't know about you, but to me that's a lot of times to forgive somebody.

Jesus illustrates this further with a parable. He compares the kingdom of heaven to a king who decided to settle accounts with his servants. One servant, who owed him an enormous sum of ten thousand talents, had no means of paying it back. Facing the sale of himself and his family, the servant pleaded for patience, promising to repay everything. Moved by compassion, the king released him and forgave the entire debt. (See Matthew 18:23–27.)

Now, you might think that having been forgiven, the servant would extend forgiveness for the rest of his life. Considering he nearly lost his wife, his children, and all his possessions, you would assume he understood the severity of his debt. What we learn from these scriptures is when we don't forgive someone, we are essentially holding a debt over them, expecting payment.

The Bible tells us that the servant who was forgiven went out and found one of his friends who owed him one hundred denarii (Matt. 18:28). To put this in perspective, let me break down these monetary values: Ten thousand talents in Jesus' day would have been equivalent to over three billion dollars, which explains why his family and possessions would need to be sold to settle such an enormous debt. In contrast, the hundred denarii owed by his friend would be nearly six thousand dollars today.[1] Clearly, there was no comparison between the two debts. You might think the sensible decision would be to forgive the smaller debt. However, unforgiveness blinds people to the forgiveness they themselves have received, which is exactly what happened with the first servant.

The Bible describes how he seized his friend and began to choke him, demanding, "Pay me back what you owe" (Matt. 18:28, paraphrased). His friend fell to the ground, pleading for patience and promising repayment but not even asking for debt forgiveness. Despite this the servant refused and had him thrown in prison until he could pay back the full amount. When other servants witnessed this, they reported it to the king (Matt. 18:29–31). The king then summoned the unforgiving servant and rebuked him, saying, "You wicked slave, I forgave you all that debt because you pleaded with me. Should you not also have had mercy on your fellow slave, in the same way that I had mercy on you?" (Matt. 18:32–33).

The Bible records that the unforgiving servant was handed over to torturers until he could repay all that was owed (Matt. 18:34). The chapter concludes with a stark warning that is especially relevant for us as believers—a warning we should take quite literally, as it was spoken directly by Jesus. He stated, "My heavenly Father will also do the same to you, if each of you does not forgive his brother from your heart" (Matt. 18:35).

There are several insights to consider here:

- **Forgiveness is not optional.** It's a fundamental expectation. The servant was judged not merely because he had been forgiven but because of his role in the king's palace. His proximity to the king meant that he was expected to emulate the king's merciful nature. His judgment was due not just to his failure to forgive but to his failure to act in a manner befitting his position.

- **Unforgiveness represents a debt held against someone.** By throwing his friend into prison for a debt that could not be paid, the servant effectively declared that his friend would always owe him, perpetuating an endless cycle of debt.

- **Unforgiveness invites torturers into our lives.** While this may not be literal, consider the torment in areas where you've held on to unforgiveness. Unforgiveness is like a cage—we lock the door believing we're protecting ourselves when in reality we're shutting everyone else out.

- **Unforgiveness leads to loneliness.** It isolates us from relationships and community, creating barriers that are hard to break down.

Do you see how prevalent this issue is in our culture today? God has forgiven us for countless transgressions—so many that we likely don't even recall all of them throughout our years of following Him. Our King has granted us mercy instead of what we deserve, yet often when it's our turn to extend that same mercy and forgiveness to others, we find reasons we can't. Much like the wicked servant, we invent every excuse to imprison our brothers and sisters in unforgiveness until we believe they have repaid their debts.

This Bible story teaches us that forgiveness is not merely about pardoning others; it's about emulating our King. Forgiveness is not just an act of duty; it is a characteristic we develop as we grow to resemble our Father. Those who fail to forgive effectively crown themselves as their own lords and kings, allowing unforgiveness, rather than Jesus, to rule their lives.

I am honored to share a story from one of my spiritual fathers, Lou Engle. Over the years I've observed Lou navigating numerous challenging situations with a spirit of forgiveness, consistently demonstrating humility even when it might have seemed justifiable to act otherwise. Here is Lou Engle's story:

Lou Engle

I want to talk about forgiving your pastors, your leaders, or people you might have worked for. All of us will be wounded in some measure concerning those who exercise authority, and I believe one of the greatest issues of every generation, but especially of the young generation, is getting offended by those who are in leadership over you. The Scripture is very clear that we need to honor those who are over us, not just the reasonable ones but the unreasonable ones, and it will always be a major test in every one of our lives. If we haven't learned to honor and forgive our parents, then

God will place others over us until we learn the lesson. Think about Joseph in the Scriptures. He is placed under Potiphar, unjustly accused, and then thrown into prison. How could you respond when these types of things take place?

People have asked me, "What is the key to the fruitfulness of your life? Was it an angel visitation? Was it an encounter that you had with Jesus?" My answer is this: "It was a moment of great testing in my life." There was a church that I was involved in, and I led a small group. We had about thirty people in our home group, and we were deeply influenced by one of the teachers. We were so drawn to this man and his prophetic, charismatic anointing.

But a church split took place, and overnight all the young men and women in my home group left the church and followed the charismatic leader. I wanted to follow this leader as well, but our pastors actually put this man under discipline. I became very upset with the pastors. I thought they were unjust and unreasonable. In fact I went to a secret meeting held by the charismatic leader; all my friends were going there, and I actually had a recording of what took place in this particular meeting.

The pastors heard about it. When I was on midnight watch with a pastor, he demanded that I turn over the recording. I did not want to, but I ended up being pressured to do so. I was upset with the leaders, yet I was still in the church, while my friends all left it. I didn't feel as if the Lord was releasing me to leave the church. I was thinking, "God, I'm so upset with these pastors. I want to leave the church." And I had unforgiveness in my heart toward them because in one sense I was also marked as part of the reason for the split.

And so one morning I was in a church service—not

of the charismatic leader who left but of the big church—and a man was giving a message from the Scripture. The passage talks about how God measures the inside of His temple, but the outside of the temple will be trampled underfoot (Rev. 11:1–2). Obviously, the Scripture meant something else and the exegesis was something else, but from it the Lord spoke very dynamically to me: "If you stay on the outside of this church, your life will be trampled under. I want you to forgive those pastors, the ones whom you are upset with and angry with. And I want you to stay in the middle of this church, and if the church sinks, I want you to sink with it. I want you to become the best intercessor for those men you don't like."

I knew it was the Lord, so I stayed and I prayed for those pastors even though I didn't like them. Little did I know that within a few months one of the pastors, Ché Ahn, would invite me to be a part of this evangelist group. And in that season he came to me and said, "Lou, if you were to go anywhere to plant a church, where would you go?"

And I said, "I would go to Los Angeles to plant a church among the Hispanics."

He replied, "I had a dream of a black man saying, 'Come to Los Angeles; there is going to be a great revival.' Lou, I'm asking you—would you pray about coming? I need a praying man."

My wife and I moved with twelve people to Los Angeles. Little did I know that out of that movement would come forth a massive mobilization movement—The Call—and all that I've done. Ché's church, Harvest International Ministries, is all over the world. Had I not forgiven my pastors, had I not stayed under their authority, and had I just run to the dream fields of prophecy without coming under leadership's authority, I would have missed the defining moment of my life. And who knows, maybe I would have missed all that's been a part of my life. You must forgive those in leadership who have wounded you; you must pray for them even as Joseph did. And if you pass that test, yes, you'll go through painful prisons and pits and Potiphar's houses, but eventually you'll find your way to the palace and lead the parade of history.

The Lord's Prayer

Our Father who is in heaven, hallowed be Your name. Your kingdom come. Your will be done, on earth as it is in heaven. Give us this day our daily bread. And forgive us our [trespasses], as we also have forgiven [those who have trespassed against us]. And do not lead us into temptation, but deliver us from evil.
—Matthew 6:9–13

What a powerful prayer, right? You've probably prayed it before many times. As believers, we love the part that says "Your kingdom come. Your will be done." Entire songs in the body of Christ are written about this. We cherish the lines "Give us this day our daily bread," "Do not lead us into temptation," and "Deliver us from evil." I'm pretty sure we've inserted people's names into that prayer, especially loving the parts about "Your kingdom" and "glory forever" (v. 13).

But what about the part that says, "Forgive us our [trespasses], as we also have forgiven [those who have trespassed against us]"? The word *trespass* in Greek suggests deviating from the right path, slipping aside. According to Blue Letter Bible and Thayer's Greek Lexicon, the Greek term used is *paraptōma*, which carries the meaning of a "lapse or deviation from truth and uprightness."[2] Before it mentions forgiving others, the Lord's Prayer focuses on our own need for forgiveness, stating, "And forgive us our debts" (v. 12). It acknowledges that we often deviate from the right way and need God's forgiveness as a gateway to forgiving others.

Have you asked God to forgive you as you forgive others? The prayer shifts when we ask God to treat us as we treat others. This prayer from Jesus was very intentional. He taught His disciples the importance of forgiving others, embedding a reminder that if we've been forgiven, we must also forgive.

Over the years, as cultures around the world intensify, forgiveness and mercy are becoming scarce. Within the church forgiveness is being redefined by cultural standards rather than biblical ones. Today's culture often defines *forgiveness* with statements such as:

- Only forgive those who have publicly repented.
- Forgiveness should not remain private; true forgiveness must be public.
- Forgiveness can be temporary; we can revoke it if anger resurfaces.
- Seeking revenge requires more strength than forgiving.
- Apologies must be accompanied by restitution, even for unrelated issues.
- Being a victim absolves one of responsibility for their actions.
- A person's identity is permanently marked by their mistakes.

I thank God that these are not the rules that He plays by. His Word remains unchanged despite shifting cultural tides. While it may be tempting to conform to popular opinion, remember, the level of mercy you extend to others will be the same mercy you receive. This aligns with what Jesus emphasized in the

Lord's Prayer about forgiving our trespasses as we forgive those who trespass against us.

Jesus and Peter on the Shore of Betrayal

In John 21 we revisit the story of Jesus after His resurrection. Just three days post-crucifixion He rose, and then we witness His meaningful reconnection with a disciple who had betrayed Him. I choose this story because it centers on Peter, a close and trusted friend of Jesus. Peter experienced events that few other apostles did, including the mountain of Transfiguration, receiving the revelation of Jesus as the Christ, and walking on water. Peter's relationship with Jesus was marked by a special favor, deeper even than the one he shared with his own brother, Andrew. There was a moment when Peter declared, "I will lay down my life for You," only for Jesus to predict that Peter would deny Him three times before the rooster crowed (John 13:37-38). This close bond between Peter and Jesus is undeniable.

Peter's denial was so severe that on the third occasion he denied Him, he even cursed and swore, openly rejecting Jesus (Matt. 26:74). What makes it all the more severe is that it was public. How do we know? Because it's documented in the Scriptures. Peter publicly denied one of his closest friends (Matt. 26:69-74).

In John 21, which I highly recommend you read in its entirety, we find a significant encounter between Jesus and Peter. First, Jesus appeared to the disciples by the Sea of Tiberias. Present were Peter, Thomas (also called Didymus), Nathanael, the sons of Zebedee, and two other disciples—seven in total. Simon Peter, eager to engage in something familiar, suggested going fishing, and the others agreed. The Bible details that they went out in a boat and fished throughout the night but caught nothing. (See John 21:1-3.)

Anyone familiar with fishing can understand the ample time it affords for reflection. Undoubtedly, Jesus' resurrection loomed large in Peter's thoughts—pondering how it was indeed true that Jesus was truly alive again. Mixed with his hope was likely a fear of being confronted for his betrayal.

As dawn broke, Jesus appeared on the beach (John 21:4). The disciples, not recognizing Him from a distance, heard Him call out, "Children, do you have any fish [to eat]?" (John 21:5, ESV). Knowing the answer, Jesus then advised them with words that likely struck a chord with Peter: "Cast the net on the right-hand side of the boat and you will find [the fish]" (John 21:6). When they complied, they indeed found their nets full (John 21:6).

The Bible recounts that the catch was abundant (John 21:6, 8). When John recognized the Lord and informed Peter, Peter immediately donned his outer garment and plunged into the sea, surely overwhelmed by a surge of emotions. Possibly fatigued from a night of fishing, Peter made his way to the shore, his mind likely filled with remorse and apprehension about the impending encounter with Jesus. (See John 21:7.)

As Peter approached the shore, the other disciples followed closely in the boat, towing the hefty catch of 153 fish, as the Gospel notes (John 21:11). Upon their arrival, they were greeted by the comforting sight of a charcoal fire with fish and bread—the same type of meal they had seen Jesus miraculously multiply before. Jesus then instructed them, "Bring some of the fish you have just caught" (John 21:9–10, NIV). Peter promptly complied, hauling the large net ashore (John 21:9–10).

The next segment of this passage that I wish to address embodies true forgiveness. The Bible teaches that "love covers a multitude of sins" (1 Pet. 4:8). Fundamentally, love is the only force capable of covering sin, offense, betrayal, pain, and our inclination toward revenge. Essentially, we understand that God is love. In my own experiences I have often found that when I've harbored unforgiveness, it was love—God—that guided me to cover those offenses within my heart. It's crucial for you to grasp that navigating the path of forgiveness is unattainable without love. What Jesus said next to Peter underscores this point. But what Jesus said was not any of the following.

- "Hey, we need to have a serious talk before we eat."
- "Hey Peter, I think you need to publicly confess what you've done and have a moment of public repentance; then I will consider forgiving you."
- "Hey Peter, what you did was wrong. I am deeply hurt and offended, and I need to get this off my chest."
- "Hey Peter, how could you do that to me? I took you to the Mount of Transfiguration and allowed you to walk on water. I may forgive you, but I will never forget that moment you denied me."
- "Hey Peter, I know you have done great things in the past, but all that is now overshadowed by this grievous mistake. I think you're permanently disqualified from being an apostle."

Can you see how this might leave a distaste in your mouth? Just imagining Jesus uttering such words might make any believer recoil, as those words are not reflective of His character at all. If we strive to emulate Jesus, why would we accept from our own lips what He would never say? Why would we condone statements from our brothers and sisters against others if we would never accept them from our Savior?

Jesus' actual words to Peter convey attributes from His character that are to be replicated in our own lives. The next four words we find in Scripture are more powerful than we may even realize; in John 21:12 Jesus said to the disciples, "Come and have breakfast." The disciples, who had all deserted Him, and Peter, who had denied Him, were all welcomed back to His table. The Bible notes that they didn't even question His identity; they knew it was Him (John 21:12). After breakfast Jesus broke what might have been an awkward silence as He addressed the proverbial elephant in the room—the unresolved offense. It's like those moments when you are in the same room with someone you've had a disagreement with; you might not verbalize it, but you hope they'll approach you just to exchange greetings, affirming that all is well.

Jesus posed a question to Simon Peter: "Simon, son of John, do you love Me more than these?" (John 21:15). Have you ever wondered what *these* in this context might refer to? Scholars suggest various interpretations. It could signify the fish Peter had just caught.[3] This would imply that Jesus inquired, "Do you love Me more than what I can provide for you?"—essentially asking if Peter loved His heart more than His provisions. Alternatively, *these* could represent the disciples, questioning if Peter loved Jesus more than his peers.[4] Regardless of the specific reference, the core question Jesus asked was profound: Do you love Me?

Peter answered swiftly, "Yes, Lord; You know that I love You" (John 21:15), likely curious about where the conversation was heading. Jesus responded, "Tend My lambs" (John 21:15). He then asked again, "Simon, son of John, do you love Me?" and Peter reaffirmed, "Yes, Lord; You know that I love You" (John 21:16). Jesus instructed him once more, "Shepherd My sheep" (John 21:16). A third time Jesus asked, "Simon, son of John, do you love Me?" (John 21:17).

I often wonder if Peter recalled the three times he denied Jesus when Jesus asked him three times if he loved Him. It's as if Jesus was allowing Peter to retract his earlier denials.

Consider the scene in Luke 22 when Peter denied Jesus (vv. 54–62). It could have unfolded differently had Peter affirmed his love by saying, "Yes, I know Jesus, and I love him." Though Peter initially failed, Jesus provided him with another opportunity to affirm his devotion by instructing him to "tend My sheep" (John 21:17).

Let me take this moment to highlight how Jesus responded naturally, spiritually, and emotionally to a man He forgave. Jesus didn't respond with aggression, even when seeking to know if Peter's heart had changed; it wasn't accusing. It didn't come with threats of further shaming. You may not realize this, but Peter's repentance was his reaffirmation of his love and his commitment to obedience in what Jesus asked. And his repentance was met with forgiveness. I encourage you to reflect on these verses and ask the Lord to show you how you have responded well and where you might need to improve in offering forgiveness. Remember all the times that Jesus has forgiven you.

What Forgiveness Is

As this chapter comes to a close, I'm sure the Lord has spoken to you about areas where you need to forgive yourself or others. Wrestling with these thoughts is good; do not be discouraged. Let God's Word be your guiding light. You might have thought you had forgiven someone, but now you realize you haven't. I want to leave you with two things: what forgiveness is and what it's not.

Growing up in the charismatic church, I answered many altar calls, making many gestures representing breakthroughs— these were powerful moments in my life. I remember one altar call when we were told to imagine the person we had an offense with, clench our fist, raise our hand, and then open our hand when we had forgiven them. This was in my teen years. I did it, and it was powerful. I wept and prayed for that person. But rarely did I leave those altar calls with practical truths for the realities I would face. Practical truths are important because they outlive experiences. While experiences validate truth, truth sustains the experience.

It is my hope that as you read the remainder of this chapter—and then in five, ten, or twenty years from now—if your heart wavers because of various situations or when new or old pains reemerge, you will first go back to the Word as your guiding light, talk to the Holy Spirit, who is your greatest Counselor, and if needed look back on this book to help you navigate these challenges.

I recently heard R. T. Kendall, an incredible preacher in his late eighties, speak on forgiveness. Seeing someone with a full head of white hair still loving and burning for God is inspiring. Not that he's perfect, but he's likely learned a lot over the years, gaining wisdom, especially from his mistakes. In his preaching at UPPERROOM Church in Dallas, Texas, he laid out a few life-changing and practical points on forgiveness. From his book *Total Forgiveness* here are ways to know that you are walking in true biblical forgiveness:

- **Tell nobody what they did.** Kendall explains how total forgiveness looks like not seeking to expose the person and what they did. We see this in the example of Joseph when he removed the Egyptians from the room so that they would not know what his brothers did (Gen. 45:1).

- **Don't let anybody be afraid of you.** Kendall explains that total forgiveness doesn't involve fear or intimidation over the other person, where you make them feel as if you have something over them or that you're holding something as blackmail. Forgiveness involves love and not fear (1 John 4:18).

- **Help them forgive themselves.** He also explains that total forgiveness looks like helping whoever wronged you forgive themselves, as you now have the desire for them to be free from guilt or shame. We see this in Joseph's interaction with his brothers in Genesis 45:5.

- **Let them save face.** Joseph's story also gives an example of how total forgiveness looks like allowing someone to save face, as we can see in Genesis 45:7–9. Forgiveness looks to preserve the other person's dignity and self-esteem.

- **Protect them from their darkest secret.** Kendall also talks about how the next part of total forgiveness involves covering the other person even from themselves. An example of this is in Genesis 45:9–13, again with Joseph and his brothers.

- **It is a life sentence.** Total forgiveness is something that you commit to for life. In Joseph's example we can see that even seventeen years later Joseph was still walking in forgiveness in Genesis 50:16–21.

- **Bless them.** And finally, Kendall talks about how total forgiveness involves blessing the other person.[5]

What Forgiveness Is Not

Just as I have listed what forgiveness is, I want to clarify what forgiveness is not, as this can be one of the most confusing aspects of forgiveness. Remember that God doesn't author confusion, and truth is our greatest boundary. Also, I encourage you, if you are struggling with unforgiveness, to stop letting social media be your source of truth. As I've said before, eliminate those who are equally offended and who bear unforgiveness from speaking into your life. I hope the following list truly helps you walk out forgiveness, and I look forward to hearing the testimonies of what Jesus will do. According to R. T. Kendall, forgiveness is not these things:

- **Approval of what they did.** Total forgiveness is not an endorsement of what they did. God does not approve of sin, but He does forgive us.

- **Excusing what they did.** Total forgiveness does not explain away the wrong.

- **Justifying what they did.** Justifying means making right or just; total forgiveness does not mean the wrong has been made right.

- **Pardoning what they did.** A pardon is a legal transaction that releases an offender from the consequences of their actions. Total forgiveness does not release the person who did the wrong from any consequences that God, not us, may allow to happen. We sin and God forgives us, but there may still be consequences.

- **Reconciliation.** Reconciliation implies a restoration of the relationship. Total forgiveness does not require reconciliation. That is a separate issue.

- **Denying what they did.** It is not suppressing or repressing the fact that a wrong occurred just so you can deal with it.

- **Blindness to what occurred.** Blindness is making a conscious choice to look the other way. It is like explaining away that a wrong actually occurred.

- **Forgetting.** Some wrongs we may never forget, but that does not mean you have not totally forgiven. You may need to remember so as not to get hurt again.

- **Pretending you are not hurt.** When we are wronged, it hurts. Hurt does not mean you have not totally forgiven. Not forgiving keeps your wound open and attracts demonic flies.[6]

I know unforgiveness can be one of the hardest things to die to, for all the reasons mentioned in this chapter. But if you don't let unforgiveness fester in your heart and kill you, you will see the trajectory of your generation shift. The generational bitterness, family feuds, and offenses with people, groups, churches, and politics will be diminished. Just as you may have grown up watching your family walk in treacherous unforgiveness, your children will see you model what Jesus did. Even if you're young and not married yet, these are foundational pieces that will shape the rest of your life.

Make It Personal

- Reflect on a time when you struggled to forgive someone. How did this affect your relationship with them and with God?

- What areas of your life has unforgiveness distorted? Write them down, and invite the Lord into those areas.

- In what ways might harboring unforgiveness be acting as a barrier to truly experiencing and embracing God's forgiveness in your life?

- How can Jesus' teaching on forgiveness, as illustrated in the parable of the unforgiving servant, transform your approach to forgiving others in your daily life?

- How can you break the cycle of unforgiveness in your family? What steps can you take to model forgiveness for future generations?

- Whom do you need to forgive? Write those names in a journal or on a piece of paper that no one will see, and ask the Lord to walk you through how to forgive them as Jesus has forgiven you.

Note: As you work through these questions, I recommend you find someone who will help keep you accountable to forgive those you need to forgive. This could be a trusted friend, family member, or pastor. Look for a strong believer you can talk to who will confidentially point you to Christ and forgiveness.

Chapter 7

SUFFERING

There is a phrase known as the "gospel of suffering," which means that in suffering there is power that draws us closer to Christ. Essentially, it's the verse that says that in our weakness His power is perfected (2 Cor. 12:9). Coming from the Protestant Western church, suffering was never something I was really taught, nor is it commonly taught across many churches and denominations. In fact we are taught to avoid suffering like the plague. Suffering is often equated with disobedience or sin, while prosperity and external monetary blessings are seen as signs of God's favor. The only problem with that is it couldn't be further from the truth, as suffering is our Savior's mark of His divine love for His creation.

Although suffering is a product of the fall and a consequence of sin in some aspects, a life laid down in sacrificial suffering, suffering that is not a consequence of our sins, is actually godly in what it produces. If we don't understand suffering, there is no way we could understand the value of our salvation. The salvation that you sing about, clap about, preach about, and wear T-shirts about came from a man who was nailed to a cross. His death was one of the most excruciating ever faced. After a long night in the Garden of Gethsemane sweating blood, after a night of betrayal, and after being arrested, He stood trial. He was sent from Pontius Pilate to Herod, then back to Pilate, and finally a death sentence was given to Jesus. On top of all He was about to endure and suffer, He did not get a good night's sleep.

Some believe that around 8 a.m. He was led away to Calvary, after being insulted, mocked, and flogged, to be crucified, dying a death that no human being should have ever endured.[1] The best depiction of this I have ever witnessed was in the movie *The Passion of the Christ*.[2] I remember when my daughter, Zoe, watched the scene of Jesus being crucified. Though controversial to some, as her father, I felt it was an important movie for her to watch so she could witness that her sin has a cost and that Jesus' suffering on the cross produced her eternal salvation. She wept as she watched the nails being driven into His hands and feet. She began to ask me questions such as, "Why did they do that, Daddy? Why didn't Jesus get down from the cross? Why didn't He fight back?" These are all valid questions, but Jesus understood suffering.

He understood what would come from His choice to willfully lay His life down. He understood the power of suffering in obedience, not suffering because of disobedience. I want to discuss in this chapter how we navigate suffering as believers because suffering with a biblical perspective can produce power in the Lord. But suffering with an unbiblical perspective can be suffocating and can choke out the very life of a believer.

The "name it and claim it" gospel, or what we know as the gospel of prosperity, has done more harm than good. It has taught people that God is most concerned with their happiness. Instead of being a Savior who saves them from their sin, He has become a genie, and they long for Him to grant their wishes like the genies in movies we've watched. A genie's sole purpose is to give the one who rubs the lamp all they want with no limitations, no hesitation, and no boundaries. But that is quite different from being a Christian who follows Jesus.

There is a difference between suffering due to our choices or the choices of others and suffering in our obedience to the Lord. Often we rebuke the devil for situations he was never involved in; it was our choices and actions that placed us in certain situations. However, there are moments when we will suffer for the gospel. If suffering were never part of our Christian life, Jesus would have never talked about it. He frequently spoke about

Suffering

how He would suffer and be betrayed as the Son of Man. He also mentioned moments where His own followers would walk through suffering. (See John 6:70–71; Mark 8:31–36; and John 15:20.)

If you look at historical and biblical records, you would likely see that most of the disciples died a death of suffering, except John the Beloved, who wrote the Book of Revelation.[3] This is not to scare you or to suggest you will die the same death but to prepare your heart to know that suffering for His name's sake will always produce a fragrance. And that suffering is an honor; it's a privilege.

- Peter was crucified upside down because he didn't consider himself worthy to be crucified right side up like Jesus. Yes, the Peter who denied Him and had some of the greatest encounters with Him suffered for the sake of Christ.

- Paul was beheaded. Yes, Paul, the one with the dramatic conversion in the Book of Acts and the one who wrote many of the scriptures we read, suffered for the sake of Christ.

- Andrew was crucified on an X-shaped cross. Yes, Andrew, the first of his brothers to follow Jesus, suffered for the sake of Christ.

- Thomas is believed to have been martyred for his faith. Yes, Thomas, the one who saw the marks of suffering on his Savior, also suffered for the sake of Christ.[4]

- Philip was arrested and cruelly put to death by the Roman proconsul. Yes, Philip, who convinced Nathaniel to join Jesus' disciples, who taught the Gentiles the gospel of Jesus, and who distributed fish and bread among the multitudes, suffered for the sake of Christ.[5]

- One report states that Matthew was stabbed to death in Ethiopia. Yes, Matthew, who was once a tax collector and left all that he had to follow Jesus, suffered for the sake of Christ.[6]

- Bartholomew is said to have been either beheaded or flayed alive. Yes, Bartholomew, responsible for bringing Christianity to Armenia in the first century, suffered for the sake of Christ.[7]

- James, the son of Alphaeus, is said to have been martyred for his faith. Yes, James, who walked with Jesus, suffered for the sake of Christ.[8]

- Simon the Zealot is said to have been martyred for his faith in Persia. Yes, Simon, who was once a revolutionist and who laid down his arms and his life, also suffered for the sake of Christ.[9]

- Matthias is said to have been stoned to death. Yes, Matthias, the apostle who took the place of Judas, also suffered for the sake of Christ.[10]

- James, the brother of John, was put to death by the sword by order of King Herod Agrippa I. Yes, James, who had seen the Transfiguration and who was closely knit into some of the most intimate parts of Jesus' life, also suffered for the sake of Christ.[11] (See Acts 12:1–2 and Matthew 17:1–2.)

I find it interesting that most of the people who were close to Jesus shared a common thread: suffering. Jesus didn't say, "The closer you are to Me, the less you will suffer," or that the higher you rise in the ranks of Christianity, the less you'll have to pay a price. So what led these men to give their lives? After all, they could have gone back to their original jobs. Some of them had families they could have returned to—remember when Jesus healed Peter's mother-in-law (Matt. 8:14–15)? They could have just lived very quiet, normal lives, living for Him but never suffering for Him or dying for Him outwardly.

There is a point of no return in the life of a believer. There is a moment that every believer experiences when you do not love your life "even unto death" (Rev. 12:11, ESV), when "to live is Christ and to die is gain" becomes your anthem (Phil. 1:21). Once enjoyed pleasures—simple ones, such as food, wine, and parties—no longer suffice in light of your inner desire to be close to God. There comes a point when you desire God above all else. Suffering is not something that we're supposed to go searching for as Christians, but it's also not something we're supposed to run from when it finds us. A lot of times the arguments against Christianity have stemmed from this word— suffering. I've heard this before: How could a loving God let people suffer?

This often refers to nonbelievers suffering from things such as sickness or injustices. I will touch on this briefly. Those sorts of sufferings are not godly sufferings; they are the consequences of sin and the fall of man. It is important to note this, as you don't want to blame God for things He is not doing. But the other sort of suffering we see is that of a believer. When things such as sickness, injustices, and even persecution happen, somehow that believer comes out on the other side looking more like Jesus.

My friend Todd once said, "If you squeeze an orange, you should get orange juice. If you squeeze an apple, you should get apple juice. If you squeeze a Christian, you should get Jesus. If you squeeze an orange and get apple juice, there is something wrong. And if you squeeze an apple and get orange juice, there is something wrong." This is exactly what suffering does to a believer—it squeezes us, and most of the time, whatever is in us is what comes out. But often it's not Jesus; it's fear, anxiety, anger, and frustration—and the list goes on.

It would be a hard theology for us to swallow that God's will could be for us to suffer, as I don't believe that God takes pleasure in our suffering. But what He does take pleasure in is when we choose Him, regardless of our suffering. Once again we look at the life of Jesus. He came down to earth with an assignment to redeem mankind, and for thirty-three years He walked around doing what He heard His Father say and going where He heard His Father tell Him to go.

The Fragrance of Suffering

And on the fateful night before the cross, we often overlook the fact that Jesus had a choice. As He conversed with God in the Garden of Gethsemane, He was trying to negotiate if there was another way. The Father didn't reply. But why do you think that is? God wasn't napping, nor was He giving Jesus the silent treatment. God was giving Him the choice. God would be cruel and unjust if He forced us into suffering. (See Mark 14:32–42 and Matthew 26:36–46, NIV.)

I have found that suffering produces a certain fragrance. Suffering has less to do with our pain and more to do with obedience to God regardless of the cost. For those of us living in the United States, we have likely never faced suffering or persecution for the sake of Christ quite like those in other countries such as China or those in the Middle East. (See Hebrews 11:36–38.) In the US we are rarely given the option of choosing Jesus or our lives. We don't face dying at the stake, with wood ready to be burned, or having a gun placed to our heads while being told to deny Jesus.

In the US, we have never really been presented with the choice Jesus had—the choice of giving God our yes one more time, knowing it will not just cost us our day, our week, or our month, but our very lives. God's will was to redeem mankind, and through His Son, His life would be laid down willfully and joyfully as a choice (John 10:17-18). This is the pinnacle of suffering: a joyful choice.

We see an example of this in the Old Testament story of Shadrach, Meshach, and Abednego. In this story we see not a rebel spirit but their desire to be obedient while living in the land of their captors, even if that obedience would lead to death. As King Nebuchadnezzar issued a decree that all should bow at the sound of the music, these three men chose not to take a knee regardless of the consequence. After being warned multiple times to bow, their relentless love, obedience, and faithfulness to the one true living God would not allow them. Then, not only were they threatened with the fire, but they were threatened that it would be heated seven times hotter than normal. (See Daniel 3:1-30.)

After the guards opening the furnace doors died, the three men might have started second-guessing their decision, but it was too late (Dan. 3:22). Their obedience had carried them this far, and regardless of what they would suffer, it would all be worth it to obey God. Do you see how obedience only makes sense when your joy is found purely in obeying? Nobody wants to suffer or feel physical pain; it's not part of our human nature. We desire comfort, security, safety, and pleasures.

As we die to ourselves, we are no longer Christians who just follow our passions, but obedience leads us, and so it did for these three men. Their hearts' cry deep inside was that God would deliver them, but their deeper cry was that even if He didn't, they still would not bow their knee. This is the heart that embraces suffering as a believer. Our external blessings have nothing to do with our obedience. Our yes to Jesus has little to do with our emotions; many times our emotions will not lead us to obey.

As they were thrown into the fire, the guards were probably amazed that there were no instantaneous screams of pain and agony. I'm not saying it wasn't hot in there, but their suffering and willingness to die invited what we know as the fourth man in the flame (Dan. 3:23–25). There is a promise in suffering—it's Him. It's Jesus. He comes every time because suffering is something we can share with our Savior.

"Christian suffering is distinctive: it arises from our union and association with Christ. It lies in those pressures, pains, and persecutions that follow when we cling to the name of and walk in the way of the Lord (Acts 14:22). Such trials and tribulations in connection with the Savior are honorable and profitable."[12]

Suffering is something that every believer from any denomination can partake in that directly gives us an understanding of our Savior. Our suffering produces a fragrance that draws Him near to us. In the instance of Shadrach, Meshach, and Abednego, their obedience—whatever the cost—and their willingness to suffer led a nation to know the one true God because Nebuchadnezzar turned and had them bow in worship to the Lord (Daniel 3:28-30).

The Suffering of Body

Some of the most joyful Christians I have ever met have been those who have suffered greatly from illnesses. I'm not making this up—some of the godliest men and women I have met have endured the greatest trials in their physical bodies. At first glance it wouldn't make sense because we often associate gratitude, thankfulness, and godliness with having everything provided for us in the natural.

But many times those who are Christian and have faced illnesses within their bodies and weaknesses for long periods develop a deep dependency on the Lord, and they possess some of the most tender hearts you will ever meet. Two of my heroes, Brian and Christy Brennt, leaders of the Circuit Riders and pioneers of The Send, both struggled with autoimmune diseases. This led Christy to lie sick in bed many days over a span of more than twenty years. Brian Brennt was one of my heroes, whose messages and genuine joy changed my life. Due to his illness he would often preach without full lung capacity.

I'm not sure of all the private conversations they had with God, but I will say that publicly, they lived with irrefutable joy in the Lord because their desire to obey Jesus was not contingent on not suffering. I never witnessed their suffering produce disobedience, grumbling, or twisted doctrine that God gave them this illness. They consistently stood by the belief that God would deliver and free them, whether on this side of eternity or the next. I don't remember once ever hearing Christy or Brian Brennt complain about the assignment God had given them. I often heard Brian be short of breath when he preached his messages, but it never stopped his passion. I never heard them say, "Why did God give me such a great assignment but not the body to fulfill it?"

They carried a perspective on suffering to be modeled after, a true kingdom perspective. As a result they experienced a deep relationship with Jesus through it all, launching tens of thousands of people into being saved, launching a whole community in Huntington Beach of young people who love Jesus, and launching stadium gatherings that have seen tens of thousands gather around the name of Christ. Oh, how the devil probably would have loved to use their suffering to jade their hearts, to allow lies to fester like, "Where is your God? If He was good, why didn't He deliver you from this suffering of your body?" But the Brennts knew that their suffering drew them close to God, and although God did not cause their sickness, He was ever present with them during it.

So what do we do when our bodies bear sickness? What do we do when suffering seems to have taken hold of us? How do we respond to God when our physical bodies are suffering?

I once sat in a message listening to a man named Dan Mohler. Mohler is mainly known for his message of grace and seeing people healed of various illnesses and diseases through the power of Jesus Christ. Dan was telling a story of how he had gone paralyzed in parts of his lower body. As the devil tried to lie to him and fill his mind with doubts, Dan's joy remained steadfast through the suffering.

The part of the story that amazed me the most was when Dan shared about a pastor coming up to him in tears one day. This pastor had known Dan's ministry, had known the different people who had been healed through Dan's ministry, and with tears in his eyes he said, "Dan, I don't understand—how did this touch you?" Dan looked him in the eyes and said, "Look at me in my eyes. Tell me if you think that this touched me." What Dan meant in that moment was that the sickness and suffering had touched his body, but it hadn't touched him. It hadn't affected his faith or his heart.

Suffering will test everything we claim to believe. It will touch parts of our lives that are still unaligned with God. Suffering will also expose things within us that we didn't know were even there. And I'm not just talking about the bad things. There are many moments when suffering will bring out the godliness of our lives. It will squeeze out of you the things we are grateful for. I was so moved by the story you're about to read. It's from an elder in our church who endured a freak accident that led her to understand who Jesus is in a whole new way, although her body was suffering.

Melissa Smith

With joy and deep gratitude that I'm alive and able to share my story, I offer it here as a testimony to the power of God. May I first say that a living hope in the gospel of Jesus Christ and in His promises—to never leave me, never forsake me, and protect me and keep me in all my ways—has been the anchor for my soul for many years through the ups and downs, the joys and sorrows of life. Little did I know when I set out on an afternoon walk a few weeks ago and wound up staring death in the face how intimately personal and true these promises would prove to be and how securely this anchor would hold.

It was a day that I will never forget, as what started as a routine walk ended in near tragedy. I was finishing my designated walking route, heading back home, and preparing to cross an intersection with a four-way stop. I first stopped to make sure that the roadway was clear and then stepped into the crosswalk to begin making my way across the street. I was almost halfway to the other side when I was suddenly struck from my left by a car traveling around twenty-five miles per hour. My body was thrown violently into the air; as I came down, the top of my head impacted the hood, and then the right side of my body slammed down very forcefully into the pavement. I remember opening my eyes the moment I hit the ground and seeing the left front tire directly in front of me, inches from my face. At this point the car was still moving, and I knew the tire was about to roll over my head. But I was injured and unable to move. I could only scream. From the depths of my being, I cried out, "Help! Please help me!" It came out as a most desperate prayer. Just then the car stopped moving. Had it rolled another inch or two, it would have crushed my head.

Suddenly, the street was filled with people. I struggled to stay conscious as voices, lights, and the wail of sirens approaching filled the air. My family was notified. The ambulance came. I was taken to the emergency room and examined, x-rayed, and scanned from head to toe. Miraculously, I did not have a single broken bone in spite of the fact that the force of the vehicle's impact with my body broke a headlight and pushed the front fender of the car in so far that the door would not open. Nor did I have a concussion or any type of head injury, even though my head struck both the vehicle and the pavement with great force. Although I was spared from broken bones and head injuries, I was admitted to the hospital with serious internal bleeding that continued for forty-eight hours and stopped just as surgical intervention was being discussed. There was a massive soft-tissue injury to both of my hips, and the recovery process from that has been extremely painful and slower than I would like. But I am healing and am expected to have no permanent damage from the injuries.

Through this very traumatic ordeal, I have seen the hand of God time and again and felt His nearness and comfort through every moment of it, especially in my times of great physical pain and emotional trauma resulting from the accident. He has been with me through the suffering, just as He promised He would be, bringing beauty from the ashes. I know beyond a shadow of a doubt that in that terrifying life-or-death moment, when I was powerless to help myself and only His intervention could change the outcome, He gave His angels charge over me (Ps. 91:11), and not one of my bones was broken (Ps. 34:19–20).

As surely as His promises are yes and amen, my faith has become sight in an even more tangible way through this experience as He covers and heals me day by day and gently carries me through to the other side.

You know, there is a beauty I have found in older saints—those who have lived out decades in their Christianity. It's something that isn't talked about much today. Older saints understand the Lord in ways others don't, depending on our season in life. Maybe it's because they've endured the various flows of life; perhaps some have experienced loss, betrayals, divorces, kids who have left the Lord, or just situations that haven't been ideal. These experiences have made them tender; their hearts remain turned toward the Lord. I have watched many older saints allow their suffering to soften even the most callous parts of who they are.

When I first read Melissa's story, I was deeply moved by her gratitude for seeing God come through and her thankfulness that even though the recovery process wasn't as she wanted, she could see Jesus through it all. I would be lying to you if I told you that you could live Christianity without suffering or that you could fast enough, pray enough, or read enough to take away suffering. But that would be unfair to you because it's not true. As you continue reading this chapter, I believe any fear of suffering you may have will diminish and the bravery to walk through it with Jesus will grow.

SUFFERING IN PERSECUTION

Is persecution biblical? And is persecution for everyone? Have you ever read Luke chapter 6, specifically verse 12 on? Jesus goes from choosing His disciples to then teaching them. He says things like, "Blessed are you who are poor, for yours is the kingdom of God" (Luke 6:20). He continues with, "Blessed are you who hunger now, for you shall be satisfied," and, "Blessed are you who weep now, for you shall laugh" (Luke 6:21). The disciples were probably thinking, "How does any of this make sense?"

But Jesus continued to teach in verse 22, saying, "Blessed are you when men *hate* [*miseó*] you, and *ostracize* [*aphorizō*] you, and *insult* [*oneidizō*] you, and *scorn* [*ekballo*] your name as evil, for the sake of the Son of Man" (Luke 6:22, emphasis added). Before I continue, the four words He uses in this beatitude are literally teaching His disciples what will happen.

If you're wondering what the word translated "hate" (*miseó*) means in the Greek, it means "to be hated."[13] "Ostracize" (*aphorizō*) means "to exclude" and "separate";[14] "insult" (*oneidizō*) means "to reproach" and "revile,"[15] and "scorn" (*ekballo*) means "to thrust...forth."[16] You can see in the beatitudes that Jesus is setting His disciples up with the proper perspective of what to expect in their faith. After giving such terrible news, He then says the oddest sentence in verse 23: "Rejoice in that day and leap for joy, because great is your reward in heaven. For that is how their ancestors treated the prophets" (Luke 6:23, NIV).

Jesus was giving them an eternal perspective of suffering and persecution. And then He goes on in verse 26. Verse 26 will put the fear of the Lord into those who desire clicks and likes and to be admired by people, who desire everyone to speak well of them and for no one to hate them. He says, "Woe to you when all men speak well of you, for their fathers used to treat the false prophets in the same way" (Luke 6:26). There is a distinctive line between those who are credible believers and prophets and those who are not. That line is, Do you need everyone to speak well of you and agree with you? Does your life have little to no resistance and pushback, or do you live a life of persecution, suffering, and pushback?

Today many people love to identify with the men and women in the Scriptures who they think had little resistance. Or they love to identify with the victorious seasons of a man or woman's life but avoid their suffering. I hear people express that they feel like Elijah calling down fire on the prophets of Baal, yet they totally miss that soon after, Elijah went through a season of deep suffering through fear and shame, hiding under a tree and wanting to die because of Jezebel's pursuit of him. (See 1 Kings 18:25–39 and 1 Kings 19:1–8.) Often we hope to identify with the aspect of calling fire down but not with the suffering he endured in his mind and heart.

Or how about this popular one: those who are told they are like Davids for their generation. Most embrace the idea of being like David in the season of his life when he swung a stone, killed a giant, got the girl of his dreams (the king's daughter), and moved up to becoming king. (See 1 Samuel 17; 18:27; and 2 Samuel 5:1–5 for some of David's early successes.) But what most fail to remember is that David fell, failed, faced the consequences of his failure, and spent time running from a king (King Saul) who wanted to kill him, all while not raising his hand against King Saul and hiding in a cave for his life. (For David's struggles and his hiding from Saul, see 1 Samuel 19:1; 24:1–22; and 23:13–29.)

The authenticity of these men, Elijah and David, and what made them who they were was their devotion to God through their suffering and the fact that not all men spoke well of them. Once again I want to make this clear: For us today, suffering is not found in saying something foolish online or doing something foolish and receiving backlash. True suffering and persecution are when we speak truth in obedience to God, with love in our hearts, and are reproached for it.

I do not want you to think that suffering was only for biblical times or was exclusive to the original church, or that people no longer endure such things today. I'm also not saying that every believer will have the same outcome in suffering, but it is important for us to prepare ourselves so that no matter what we face, we are ready to die for the faith. As I often say, no martyr who ever gave their life died at the moment of their physical death; rather, the martyr who has died laid their life down long before they died.

What Is a Martyr?

Do you know what the word *martyr* means? The Greek word *martus*, from which we derive *martyr*, means "a witness."[17] Why would a term used to identify our death for Christ mean "witness"? In Revelation 12 the Bible says, "And they overcame him [the enemy] by the blood of the Lamb and by the word of their testimony, and they did not love their lives to the death" (v. 11, NKJV). Our lives, if lived according to Scripture—if we lay them down, deny ourselves, and die daily to our old man and our sinful nature—are witnesses. But not loving our lives unto physical death is also a witness.

Did you know that Scripture says the blood of the martyrs cries out for justice? The Bible states in Revelation 6:9–10, "When he opened the fifth seal, I saw under the altar the souls of those who had been slain because of the word of God and the testimony they had maintained. They called out in a loud voice, 'How long, Sovereign Lord, holy and true, until you judge the inhabitants of the earth and avenge our blood?'" Those who have died for Christ still have a voice, and their lives will be vindicated by the Lord.

When I had just gotten saved, I came across a book called *Jesus Freaks: Stories of Those Who Stood for Jesus, the Ultimate Jesus Freaks* by DC Talk and Voice of the Martyrs.[18] I was deeply impacted by the stories I read.

I can't tell you how many times, in my early days of following God, I thought I was suffering because I had Bible debates with individuals. I thought I was suffering because I had disagreements with the sound technician when I was leading worship or because someone disagreed with the way I interpreted

Scripture. As I began to read stories about real martyrs—people who actually died for their faith—my heart was shattered. It shattered from stories about people such as John Bradford, Laurence Saunders, John Brown, John Willfinger, Redoy Roy, Reverend Wau, Ahmad El-Achwal, Jiang Zongxiu, Rami Ayyad, Manuel Camacho, Rocio Pino, Mathayo Kachili, the twenty-one Christians martyred by ISIS, Pastor Gideon Periyaswamy, and those involved in the Surabaya church bombings, to name just a few.[19]

Not everyone will have the honor of receiving the death of a martyr. I do say honor because that's what it is to lay our lives down in such a manner. I thought it would be most appropriate to end this chapter by honoring those who have laid down their lives for the sake of the gospel. May we always continue to pray for those being persecuted in this way across the body of Christ, and may we embrace suffering as an essential part of our Christianity.

Make It Personal

- Do you struggle to see suffering as part of the Christian life? If so, why? If not, what has shaped your perspective?

- Has suffering affected the way you see God? If so, how? Have your views changed after reading this chapter?

- How do your personal experiences with suffering align with or challenge the idea that suffering can draw us closer to Christ and reveal His power?

- In what ways have teachings about prosperity and avoiding suffering affected your perception of God's role and intentions in your life?

- How does the example of Jesus' suffering and sacrifice challenge your own approach to enduring hardships and trials?

- What does the concept of suffering as a privilege or honor mean for your own faith and commitment to following Christ?

- How can the stories of modern and historical martyrs inspire or inform your understanding of suffering and persecution in your own faith journey?

Chapter 8

DISAPPOINTMENT

WHAT DO YOU do when your pain feels more overwhelming than your faith? What do you do when what you prayed for doesn't just go unanswered but the unthinkable happens? What happens when you see others receive God's breakthrough and you are left with disappointment?

In our disappointments lie the choice to either fall away or continue to follow Jesus when we are met with great letdowns. I have heard these phrases over the years: "If God was good, then…" or "If God was real, then…" We have attached His goodness and, even worse, His existence to our senses of fulfillment. This means that our disappointments become indicators that He must not be real. We have sometimes linked our happiness and everything working out for us to God's nature. Conversely, we have attributed our pain to His actions. We have even associated our struggles with fellow believers as being the Father's fault.

Disappointment is by far an underestimated tool in the devil's hand. He uses it as a blinding light to point us away from God. Disappointment, meant to lead us into conversations with God, is a wedge that works its way into the middle of our relationship with God. In our disappointments we often turn to friends, podcasts, or therapists to try to make sense of things that only God can bring peace to.

Situations like deaths and sicknesses become our ammunition either to fall away from or to follow more fervently after Jesus. These events, if not seen through the lens of faith and endurance, will create a view of God as destructive as leaving the faith. Your faith is a home in which you will rest securely knowing your redemption, but its foundation is your views and beliefs. This is why we are to worship the God who made us in His image, not the God we made in ours.

"Fall or follow" is a phrase that came up in a discussion I had about handling disappointments as a Christian. I have witnessed many believers whose faith was shipwrecked because they didn't know how to process disappointment. The Bible says that nothing can separate us from the love of God, but it never says we can't willfully walk away from Him (Rom. 8:38–39). I believe more people walk away because of disappointment than we realize. If anybody knew of mistreatment from religious leaders, it was our Savior, Jesus. Sadly, many have chosen not to follow Him anymore because of their own brokenness and the brokenness of others. We are now at a pivotal time when we will either fall or follow.

Our default reactions when we face disappointments or letdowns—or when we think we heard God but our experiences don't align with what we heard—are often to ignore what happened or to throw a lot of Christian jargon at the situation instead of really facing the realities of what we went through. In this chapter I am primarily referring to those whose disappointment results from the sensation that God has let them down based on the promises found in His Word. Here are some examples of the types of disappointment I am *not* referring to:

- You prayed for God to have you marry an actor, and it didn't happen.

- You asked God to prove Himself by telling Him to knock down a picture from the wall, and that didn't happen.

- You asked God to give you a new pair of shoes for your birthday, and that didn't happen.

Disappointment

Yes, these situations can cause us to feel disappointed at the moment, but they don't necessarily lead to a state of deep disappointment within us. These examples don't fall within the context of God's will and promises as described in His Word.

Throughout the remainder of this chapter I will share stories from several friends of mine who share about deep disappointments they have experienced in their lives and how they overcame them. We will also look at the Scriptures to guide us to a healthy place when we are walking through disappointing seasons. My hope is that you come to realize how disappointment places two choices before us as Christians: We can either fall away or follow Jesus. Every legend in the faith faces this reality.

Life has a way of throwing curveballs that we never expected. Allow me to share what some of these curveballs can look like. Better yet, I'll list a few situations that you may be able to relate to that are genuinely disappointing situations we face as believers:

- Someone you love gets sick. You pray for them, and they are not healed.

- Someone you love was terminally ill; you felt as if God said He was going to heal them, but they ended up passing away.

- You felt as if the Lord was going to restore a relationship or friendship, but it turned south, and you haven't spoken to the person since.

- You felt that God was going to turn around a situation you were in, but instead you had to walk through it.

- You felt as if God was going to take away all your depression and suicidal thoughts at the prayer meeting, but you left still battling them.

- You feel as though you should have been free from that addiction you were in, but years later you find yourself still repenting.

We can get really technical here and delve into all the reasons that we think someone didn't get free—I've heard a lot of them. They didn't pray enough, they didn't fast enough, they didn't read their Bible enough, they weren't serious about their faith, they left open doors to things in the spirit, they didn't break off generational curses from ten generations ago, or they're not tithing or giving. Whatever reason we give, the outcome is the same: The person who is going through whatever they are facing is left with disappointment.

So what do we do when faced with disappointing situations? What do we do when what we thought we believed takes a turn for the worst? How do we navigate deep sorrow and anger in these moments, and how do we start believing in God again when we feel He didn't come through the last time?

I remember hearing a message once about the deep sorrow that the disciples experienced after Jesus, in John 15, gives them the parable about the vine, the vinedresser, and the fruit. He commands the disciples to love one another, and in verse 13 He says, "Greater love has no one than this, that one lay down his life for his friends" (John 15:12–13). Jesus was obviously speaking about His death. He continues to teach them, saying things like, "Remember the word that I said to you" (John 15:20). Implying that He would be leaving, He then says to them in verse 26, "When the Helper comes, whom I will send to you from the Father, that is the Spirit of truth" (John 15).

Then, in John 16 He says, "But now I am going to Him who sent Me; and none of you asks Me, 'Where are You going?' But because I have said these things to you, sorrow has filled your heart" (vv. 5–6). There is no place prior in the Gospels where we see sorrow filling the hearts of Jesus' disciples until this moment. Do you ever wonder why sorrow filled their hearts?

Jesus was foretelling His death, which would have been a great disappointment for His disciples. This wasn't just because the greatest leader and rabbi in human history was going to die but because all their hopes and beliefs were likely being shattered. The Messiah, the Savior, or, as Peter wrote, the Christ, the Anointed One of God—His storyline was not following what they wanted. They had hoped for Jesus to take His rightful place as King and redeem everything. But now the disappointing words—that He would have to send the Holy Spirit in His place because He would no longer be there—were starting to settle in. The thought of not having Jesus just a whisper away or a stone's throw away was heartbreaking to the point that Jesus said, "Sorrow has filled your hearts."

Deep grief filled their hearts from that moment. Throughout the following chapters that John wrote, there was no indication that the sorrow had left. But until His actual death, there was probably still hope that something could change. There must have been. Peter tried to rebuke Jesus in Matthew 16 after Jesus explained that He would go to Jerusalem; suffer many things at the hands of elders, chief priests, and teachers of the law; and then be killed and raised on the third day (Matt. 16:21–22). Peter's last-ditch effort was to tell Jesus, "Never, Lord!" in verse 22: "This shall never happen to you!" (Matt. 16). There was always hope that although Jesus had told them what would happen, it wouldn't happen that way.

The night after Jesus died on the cross, the sorrow of each disciple probably reached a pinnacle. And on the third day, that sorrow had driven out their belief. You know the story if you've read your Bible. The women came back with the report of His resurrection, and the majority of them didn't believe it because their disappointment had led to deep sorrow, and their deep sorrow had led to unbelief. The danger of disappointment, if not dealt with, is that it leads believers to unbelief. Enough disappointment over a period of time, if not taken captive and nourished with the Word of God, can lead even the strongest Christians to unbelief. After all, I don't know any other Christians who actually physically walked with Jesus other than the apostles, yet even they found themselves in this place.

A story that Pastor Michael Miller shared about his friend's passing, and the deep grief and disappointment he navigated, is one that I never forgot. I am honored that he would share this story in this book, and I know that through it those who have found disappointment in such deep ways will meet Jesus.

Michael Miller

I often tell this story because disappointment happens. Things don't always turn out the way you thought they would, especially when you really start to believe God for big things. Have you ever believed God for something, and it didn't turn out? What we do sometimes, and often, is we just put a bandage over it; we ignore it; we grit our teeth. And then we just start shouting at mountains, but it's really not from the place of faith. It's just because it's something that we've learned to do. And it's not from relationship; it's not from connection; it's not from a real, pure place. It's just like how we shout at mountains because we're charismatic, or we pray these prayers because we've seen someone else do it. But it's not this intimate heart connection with Him; it's not from that source.

I got there, and I was there. I was believing for healing in Christ. A lot of people believe in healing—but they didn't believe in healing as I was believing for it. It was like if you were sick in the church, you came to me—I was known as the guy that you needed to come to because I believed that God would heal. I was walking in this real purity of the revelation of Jesus as a healer. So there was a young man who was sick with cancer in Dallas; he was nineteen years old, and his name was Willy. Willy was diagnosed with some rare form of cancer, and he had it most of his life. He had a dream, and in the dream his mom called a Church of Christ and asked for the pastor to come to the house. And the Church of Christ pastor laid hands on Willy, and Willy got up from a sickbed.

Now, that has to be God if you know anything about the Church of Christ. So I got this phone call, and actually, Willy's mom said she called a Church of Christ and they said, "We don't really have a ministry like this and fully believe that, but let me send you to this other church." The church was kind of the progressive of the Church of Christ, and when she called the secretary there, they sent it to me, and I answered the phone. On the other end of the line there's this desperate mother, and I'm like, "Snap. Yes. I'll be there." So I immediately went over, and I developed a relationship with this amazing young, nineteen-year-old kid, and we began praying for him, and God started moving on him.

He was a freshman at the University of Texas, and he had to come back halfway through his fall semester because the cancer came back. By the end of Christmas it was back in remission, and he was planning on going back to school. At the end of January he was in Austin and he had a major relapse with cancer, so he moved back to Highland Park. We just continued to pray, continued to pray, and continued to pray, and we saw his numbers go up and down. But man, I was so full of faith that God was going to heal this young man.

Long story short, in May 2006, I believe it was, Willy died. His cancer came back so aggressively. It took us all by surprise, but within a two-week period I went from thinking this young man was going to be healed to this man is dead. He was a young boy, a vibrant young man, and then I was devastated. I was completely devastated. I remember telling the Lord, "You have a really sick sense of humor to have a mother have this young man who dreamt about a pastor. And You call me, and You send me over there. I did my part, but You didn't do Yours." I was honest with Him.

I had to go to church because I was paid to. But when people would stand up and sing and raise their hands, I would cross my hands. I would sit down, and I was in the back corner. I was ticked and frustrated with the Lord, and I remember the Lord said, "Son, you need to deal with this. You need to deal with this offense. You're offended at you." I could not deny reality. I was just letting the Lord have it, and I knew my heart was there. I told the Lord and admitted this to Him, and I stayed to the back corner. I fell on the ground, and I said, "Only You can shepherd me through this. Only You can, and so I can trust my heart to You. Will You shepherd me through this?" That was on a Saturday night. Willy's funeral was the next day, on a Sunday afternoon.

I was driving down the highway to go to his funeral. It was a massive funeral in Highland Park and was Presbyterian. So we were on the way, and as I was driving, I remembered I had a dream the night before. In the dream I was playing golf, and I love golf. I was playing the Dallas National, and I really love the Dallas National. The Dallas National is one of the nicest courses in Texas. You have your caddies, and they have these comfort stations on about every three holes, where you can go in and get anything that you want. It's a really, really nice place. It's amazing. So I had finished my round, and I was coming off the eighteenth green, and Willy, this young man who had died, was driving up on a cart.

The entire time I knew him he didn't have hair because of the chemo. But in this dream he had really long, flowing hair. He was a big guy, but most of the time when I knew him, he was very skinny because of the chemo. But in the dream he was fit, and he walked up to me. He gave me the biggest hug, and he said that was an amazing round that I played at the Dallas National. Then he said, "Do you see up in the pro shop? The head pro is up there, and he's requesting to talk to you."

So I gave Willy a hug, and I walked up. I remember the head pro shop had these clouds hitting the windows, and it overlooked the course. I walked into the pro shop, and it was shiny. It was glowing. The head pro turned and looked at me, and I remember these piercing eyes as he said, "I'm so thankful that you played the Dallas National today." But he said, "I want to tell you—this wasn't a normal round at the Dallas National. Although you played well, I want you to know that it wasn't a standard round or a normal round." He said, "I want to give you two options. You can take any of these shirts." They were all these really legitimate golf shirts, like amazing golf shirts. I love good golf shirts. One of the ones he was offering me to choose was this micro-fabric stuff that absorbs your sweat, and it was a really light baby-blue color and said "Dallas National" on it. I looked at the shirts, and then he was like, "Or you can play another round."

In my dream I knew I was gonna play another round. I grabbed the ticket. I said, "I'm gonna play another round," and I walked out. And as I was driving to Willy's funeral, I was mad at God and frustrated for the process that I'd been through because I didn't believe it was His will for a nineteen-year-old boy to die of cancer, especially in light of his dream, his revelation, and all the stuff that we walked through. As I shared my dream with Lorisa, I immediately got revelation, and the revelation was this: The Dallas National to me is heaven on earth. It is heaven on earth. So it's heaven on earth, and our commission is to bring heaven to earth. Here I had contended and played this round with Willy, and Willy drove down the green healthy and whole.

I think this is heaven's perspective of where he's at today. Willy told me that the head pro wanted to talk to me. Who is the head pro? The head pro is Jesus Himself. I walked off, and I talked to Jesus, and Jesus, with His piercing eyes, gave my heart two options. My heart's options were: I could just take a souvenir and wear it because this is just what happens when nineteen-year-olds get cancer. Or I could take the ticket, and I could contend again, knowing this wasn't a normal round for heaven coming to earth. My heart was liberated. My heart, because Jesus shepherded my heart through the disappointment and through the pain, got a resurrected perspective of the Lord, based on my circumstance. I could itemize His resurrection to what my heart went through.

My heart—although it was in pain, although I would grieve, and although it would go through so much in the days to come with the family and others—had a new perspective to see my situation through the resurrection. This perspective brought healing, enlargement, and a capacity to behold the mystery of why Willy died. But it also brought the courage to contend again for nineteen-year-olds to get healed of cancer. And I've actually seen at least two teenagers that I know healed of cancer since that time. But if I was wearing the T-shirt and had developed some weird theology that's not based on the Bible, I wouldn't have had the courage to enter into those situations again. I believe the Lord is resurrecting our hearts from dead, disappointed places so that we can contend again and believe again. And I believe that this generation that's out there, that's walking away from the church, is looking for hearts that actually *believe in* what they believe. And they are looking for those who demonstrate the power behind that.

Facing Disappointing Situations

Our pain can drive out our faith faster than we grow in it. Have you ever seen someone who followed God—who loved God and even preached and did mighty works in His name—fall away faster than you could have imagined? Deep sorrow replaces the place in their heart that God once occupied; pain now takes that place. The place where they worshipped and thanked God, the place where they once gave Him glory, is now substituted with their heart, mind, and soul being fixed on the issue before them. Their thankfulness becomes grumbling. Instead of glory ascribed to His name, it becomes accusations like, "That's not what You said."

And who God is to us is who He'll be through us. Our lives begin to preach our broken views of God, without words. With this in mind I share another story, from a friend who navigated such a troubling time of disappointment at the sudden loss of his father.

Tim Bruce

The story is still unfolding for me today. As I write this, it was only a year ago that everything happened. So I'll do my best to articulate what transpired, where I am now, and how I've overcome the challenges of 2023.

As I was preparing for my wedding, excitement filled me—I had a secret to share with my wife. My dad would be my best man. Unbeknownst to him, he pondered the possibility of officiating the ceremony. Little did he know I wanted him by my side, as he had been throughout my entire life—present, kind, full of love, and always guiding me toward Jesus. Truly, he was my best friend.

Amid these preparations, I was on a ministry tour when a life-shattering call came out of nowhere—my father had stopped breathing. In a sudden and heartbreaking moment my father was gone. This became the most unexpected, shocking, and painful event in my life so far. I didn't know how to cope. Tears streamed down my cheeks from a depth of pain I'd never felt.

He had called me that morning, and I hadn't answered. The regret tore me apart. How I wished to hear his voice one more time, to share one more laugh.

I won't claim expertise on grief in this story, but I want to share something beautiful to prevent the enemy from gaining a foothold on the vulnerable. A few weeks later I had a dream—in it I discovered that my father was alive. The revelation left me blown away, shocked, and confused. He didn't reveal his presence, but I asked him to pick me up, and he was nearby at a grocery store. His voice began to cut out as I was speaking with him over the phone in the dream, so I became concerned. I checked my phone to see where his location was, and he was still moving toward me. He turned onto a street that connected to where I was, and the name of that street was "Communion." As he moved toward me, the dream ended.

Upon waking, sadness lingered for not seeing him. However, the dream returned to me weeks later while driving, and the Lord spoke to me, saying,

"Communion is your access to your dad." For the first time since that morning, a wave of joy hit me. I realized that because of the blood of Jesus poured out on the cross, I would one day be reunited with my father. He was currently watching my life with joy, even though I couldn't see him.

The dream wasn't just about my father; it pointed to the access the blood of Jesus provides to the heavenly Father. My longing for my dad mirrored my longing for God, and through Jesus' blood I could draw near to Him in my deepest pain. This revelation became my source of strength and overcoming.

There were no tips or tricks, no strategies to stay strong during grief—just the blood of Jesus. When life takes an unexpected turn, it's not about giving yourself a motivational speech. It's about understanding that through the blood of Jesus you have access to the Father, who holds your entire life.

In times of uncertainty or surprise, drawing near to God is not about figuring everything out or knowing why it's happening. It's about intimacy. My father's main goal in life was to make God smile—he was not driven by success or wealth but by a consuming desire to honor God through a life and friendship with Jesus.

In that same understanding and lifestyle, my father conquered, and I will conquer by the blood of Jesus. I will draw near to God and live a life of friendship. In that I will conquer.

Navigating Your Emotions Through Disappointment

In Tim's story about his father there are some things that I personally have taken away, especially since I knew who his father was. I remember the day Tim described as if it were yesterday. I recall receiving a message from him asking for prayers for his father and, shortly after, another message saying that he was gone. A wave of disbelief, disappointment, and questions filled my heart as I thought about a friend, whom I had known for the past five years, losing someone so near and dear to him.

I watched from a different perspective how my friend navigated such a troubling time of disappointment. I saw him waver through sorrow, disappointment, and anger, but never in his love for God. I'm not saying he didn't have questions for God, but he never allowed his disappointment to make him question God's very nature. I believe what his father had instilled in him through his walk with God became an anchor in his life.

I stood there the day Tim got married. Looking over to the left, I saw his mother and sisters, and an empty chair with flowers where his father would have sat. As their ceremony was coming to a close and we were blessing him, over the speakers we played the last blessing that Tim's father had ever given him. I watched him weep, and although there were probably many questions in his heart that day, his assurance, strength, and foundation were in the Lord.

Inevitably, disappointment will always touch our emotions. It will create a million scenarios of what could have, should have, and would have been. Disappointment has a funny way of leading us back to Jesus if we let it. When it comes to people who have passed in our lives as Christians, we know this truth: We never truly die. Our bodies are mere space suits that house our spirits.

Tim also mentioned the blood of Jesus. In His blood and through His blood, even the most disappointing moments are washed. To a nonbeliever, none of this will make sense. The Bible states, "For the word of the cross is foolishness to those who are perishing, but to us who are being saved it is the power of God" (1 Cor. 1:18). Overcoming disappointment is supernatural. It takes the cross to overcome those areas. And disappointment doesn't discriminate. It never picks the proper time to come. In fact it always seems to time itself at the worst possible moment in your life.

Navigating our emotions through it can feel as though we're in a tiny boat in a massive ocean during a storm. We quickly turn to survival mode, trying to protect and preserve ourselves from further pain. Self-preservation often becomes our shield and is an outcome of disappointment. We distance ourselves from areas of disappointment, from the people or groups we were disappointed by, and we even sometimes question or abandon a theology of God we once believed because of a situation or scenario.

I once heard that our emotions are incredible followers but terrible leaders. Disappointment will sometimes try to take the hand of Jesus from the steering wheels of our lives and hand them over to our emotions. In these seasons we must walk by faith and not by sight. (See 2 Corinthians 5:7.) The emotions we sometimes feel with disappointment can be

- nervousness to trust,
- worry or anxiety,
- regret that we ever trusted,
- feeling excluded,
- insecurity,
- embarrassment for how we believed God,
- terror to try to believe Him again,
- hesitancy to move forward,
- confusion,
- anger, which can lead to hate and rage when undealt with,

- hostility toward the Word of God or people wanting to speak truth, and
- feeling trapped between what we know is true and what we just experienced.

All these feelings are very normal for a human being. Nowhere have I read that Jesus is scared of our emotions. But He does desire to walk us through them. If our emotions were created, then we were never meant to follow them; we are meant to follow the Creator.

Believing God Again

Believing God again can be hard if the concrete of disappointment has settled, and sometimes the only way to lay a new foundation is to completely break apart the old. While that process may be painful, it might be the only option. Believing God again often means facing the realities of our disappointments, embracing them, and embarking on the journey to trust God again. It means accepting that being made new sometimes requires dying to and removing what is old.

Have you ever wondered why the people of Israel wandered for forty years after God delivered them? Imagine the disappointment the Israelites had in God, crying out daily for deliverance but being enslaved for 430 years (Exod. 12:40–41). Not only were they enslaved, but they were also treated cruelly, used only to build an empire that was not theirs. Imagine their disappointment, not only in their circumstances but also deeply ingrained within them.

I once heard that God will use situations as hooks to pull out of us something we did not know was still in us. God delivered the people of Egypt from the hand of Pharaoh through Moses, who unleashed plagues as commanded. He unleashed plagues of turning water to blood, of frogs, boils, hail, locusts, and the death of firstborn sons, to name a few (Exod. 7–12).

God began the deliverance of His people, and eventually they crossed the Red Sea. He did not just want to deliver them from slavery and Pharaoh's hand. God also wanted to restore the years of disappointment that slavery had caused. He even willed them to take articles of silver, gold, and clothing from the Egyptians (Exod. 12:35–36), restoring what they had lost. However, God never intended for them to take their disappointment into the Promised Land.

The journey probably came with a wave of emotions. As they followed Moses, there were likely flickers of hope that their slavery had ended, only to be met by Pharaoh's chariots and disappointment once again. There was likely also great unbelief and fear because, in a twisted way, disappointment becomes a place of false safety. We think if we stay there, we can't be disappointed again. In Exodus 14 we see the Israelites' disappointment quickly resurfacing as Pharaoh drew near.

> As Pharaoh drew near, the sons of Israel looked, and behold, the Egyptians were marching after them, and they became very frightened; so the sons of Israel cried out to the Lord. Then they said to Moses, "Is it because there were no graves in Egypt that you have taken us away to die in the wilderness? Why have you dealt with us in this way, bringing us out of Egypt? Is this not the word that we spoke to you in Egypt, saying, 'Leave us alone that we may serve the Egyptians'? For it would have been better for us to serve the Egyptians than to die in the wilderness."
> —Exodus 14:10–12

We can see from this verse that their disappointment quickly resurfaced. They began to question God's goodness and faithfulness, doubting whether they would actually live and wondering if their grave would be where they stood. They then asked why they were brought out of Egypt only to die in the wilderness, instead of being left to continue serving the Egyptians in slavery. Do you see what disappointment does? It lies to you. It tells you it's better to stay in bondage than to trust freedom. Watch as the story unfolds and God begins to deliver His people from slavery, bondage, and disappointment.

Moses' response to their fear and disappointment, and the promise of what the Lord would do:

> But Moses said to the people, "Do not fear! Stand by and see the salvation of the LORD which He will accomplish for you today; for the Egyptians whom you have seen today, you will never see them again forever. The LORD will fight for you while you keep silent."
> —EXODUS 14:13–14

The Lord instructs Moses on how deliverance would come:

> Then the LORD said to Moses, "Why are you crying out to Me? Tell the sons of Israel to go forward. As for you, lift up your staff and stretch out your hand over the sea and divide it, and the sons of Israel shall go through the midst of the sea on dry land. As for Me, behold, I will harden the hearts of the Egyptians so that they will go in after them; and I will be honored through Pharaoh and all his army, through his chariots and his horsemen. Then the Egyptians will know that I am the LORD, when I am honored through Pharaoh, through his chariots and his horsemen."
> —EXODUS 14:15–18

God protects His people during their deliverance:

> The angel of God, who had been going before the camp of Israel, moved and went behind them; and the pillar of cloud moved from before them and stood behind them. So it came between the camp of Egypt and the camp of Israel; and there was the cloud along with the darkness, yet it gave light at night. Thus the one did not come near the other all night.
> —Exodus 14:19–20

The miracle of God doing the impossible (God did not part the seas instantly—He did it overnight):

> Then Moses stretched out his hand over the sea; and the Lord swept the sea back by a strong east wind all night and turned the sea into dry land, so the waters were divided. The sons of Israel went through the midst of the sea on the dry land, and the waters were like a wall to them on their right hand and on their left. Then the Egyptians took up the pursuit, and all Pharaoh's horses, his chariots and his horsemen went in after them into the midst of the sea. At the morning watch, the Lord looked down on the army of the Egyptians through the pillar of fire and cloud and brought the army of the Egyptians into confusion. He caused their chariot wheels to swerve, and He made them drive with difficulty; so the Egyptians said, "Let us flee from Israel, for the Lord is fighting for them against the Egyptians."
> —Exodus 14:21–25

God destroys the enemies of His people:

> Then the Lord said to Moses, "Stretch out your hand over the sea so that the waters may come back over the Egyptians, over their chariots and their horsemen."

> So Moses stretched out his hand over the sea, and the sea returned to its normal state at daybreak, while the Egyptians were fleeing right into it; then the LORD overthrew the Egyptians in the midst of the sea. The waters returned and covered the chariots and the horsemen, even Pharaoh's entire army that had gone into the sea after them; not even one of them remained. But the sons of Israel walked on dry land through the midst of the sea, and the waters were like a wall to them on their right hand and on their left.
> —EXODUS 14:26–29

The deliverance from disappointment:

> Thus the LORD saved Israel that day from the hand of the Egyptians, and Israel saw the Egyptians dead on the seashore. When Israel saw the great power which the LORD had used against the Egyptians, the people feared the LORD, and they believed in the LORD and in His servant Moses.
> —EXODUS 14:30–31

You would think that after seeing such a great miracle, there would never be a question, a doubt, or a fear, let alone ever a disappointment that God couldn't do something or that He wouldn't. But as we've read, we can see that although God delivered His people from Egypt, Egypt was still very much inside of them. When disappointment settles for too long in our hearts, it becomes our culture. Sadly, it becomes our belief system.

There might be many things you've gone through that have created disappointment, but it's important that as you continue to follow Jesus, you let Him drown those disappointments just as He did the Egyptians. Laying down our lives daily and picking up our crosses also means laying down yesterday's disappointments. There comes a point when we want to believe God again—believe His promises, His goodness, and that He works for the good of those who love Him (Rom. 8:28). We want to know that although He didn't cause the issue or the problem, He can surely see us through it.

I've seen disappointment take out so many believers or keep them just attending weekly services but not really living out all that God has for them. I know there is a wave of grace and mercy coming to the body of Christ to lead us out of things we've been enslaved to.

I even feel right now that some of those reading this have disappointments and struggles with sin that have lingered since childhood. There may be disappointment that God can set other people free but not you. But just as Moses came representing the Lord, proclaiming deliverance to the Israelites who thought slavery would be their fate forever, I proclaim to you that deliverance is coming from your disappointments. You will find freedom, and although you might have spent years wandering, there is a promised land that God wants you to walk into.

Make It Personal

- How have your experiences of disappointment with the Lord or the church affected your relationship with Christ?

- Have you seen or experienced disappointment in your spiritual journey that led you to question God's goodness or existence? How did you navigate those moments?

- What disappointments did you learn or inherit from your family, your friends, or the environment you grew up in that you would like to submit to Jesus?

- In what areas of life would you like to exchange your disappointment for faith again? Maybe it's believing God can heal or that reconciliation is possible. Don't limit your list. I encourage you to list those disappointments in a journal or on a piece of paper and then write the related promises of God next to them.

- How can you shift your perspective to view disappointment not as a sign of God's absence but as an opportunity for deeper intimacy with Him? What practical steps can be taken to maintain faith during times of significant letdown?

- What are some strategies for rebuilding trust in God after experiencing deep disappointment or unmet expectations? How can you ensure that your emotions do not override your commitment to Christ?

Chapter 9

COMPLAINING

WORDS ARE POWERFUL. They have the power to destroy or create. Complaining is very dangerous. The first thing that it starts to kill is the person it's coming from, and then everyone else. So how should we be conducting ourselves as believers? I came from a family where complaining seemed to be as common as air, whether we were driving in traffic and there were too many people on the road or the food at the restaurant wasn't good enough. Complaining was part of our everyday conversation. When I became a Christian, all that began to change. I started recognizing how Christianity and complaining could not coexist and how Jesus had saved my heart and also wanted to save my tongue.

Yes, complaining has been a silent killer of Christians for centuries, as complaining rarely starts with your words; it starts in your heart and in your mind. Complaining is an underlying issue that rarely goes away unless it is dealt with head-on through the Word of God. Unlike gossip, which is outward to others, complaining is more of an inward voice that a lot of times speaks directly to you, causing you to be critical of others and critical of yourself while robbing your joy. Complaining oftentimes even masks itself in religion. Complaining can be hard to pinpoint as a sin (Phil. 2:14). This is because we feel it's not affecting anybody but ourselves. However, the real person it's affecting is you.

We were never called to live our Christianity with and through complaining (Phil. 2:14). We will soon discuss the power of our words and how often we think that verse, Philippians 2:14, means just the words we speak externally. But that couldn't be further from the truth, because the words we speak internally to ourselves are just as powerful. Remember, you are the number one voice you listen to because you are with yourself 24/7. You are not always with your pastor, your leader, your mentor, your spiritual father, your spiritual mother, or even your godly community or church, but you are always with yourself. Just as Jesus brought a whip and cleaned out the temple, He wants to clean out complaining from our temple. (See John 2:15–17.)

The Bible says in Philippians 2:14–15 to "do all things without grumbling or disputing, that you may be blameless and innocent, children of God without blemish in the midst of a crooked and twisted generation, among whom you shine as lights in the world" (ESV). Complaining is essentially an internal dispute that never goes away. It wages war with you, preventing you from enjoying the very things that God has placed in front of you. Our internal complaining often looks, sounds, and feels like the following:

- pinpointing the smallest faults in every scenario
- observing how something didn't go our way instead of seeing the ways it worked out
- dwelling on past events and comparing them to current situations
- often being left with regret at the end of the day, as complaining causes us to miss out on things we can never get back
- aggressive outbursts or passive, subtle comments made under the breath
- use of disgusted facial expressions and body language along with words

- trying to justify our complaints by saying we simply desire a situation to be better
- denying that we complain and saying we're just being real
- rarely being able to take correction

These traits, if unchecked, can often become strongholds in our lives. A stronghold, according to the Word of God, is a fortress, which isn't bad if what you're fortifying is truth (Ps. 18:2). But oftentimes strongholds are twisted by the devil and used to fortify lies in our lives. Whereas the Lord is meant to be our stronghold, as it says in Psalm 27:1, we often allow other things to become strongholds. Complaining often becomes a stronghold that keeps out the truth that the Word of God, or men and women of God, would bring. Complaining also likes to hide subtly for years until a great offense or situation occurs, and then like a dam that's been broken, it floods out of the mouth of a believer.

Complaining—unlike offense, bitterness, and even deconstruction—often hides itself in a unique way. Complaining will disguise itself as being a problem solver or wanting to help other people, yet the critical spirit behind it leaves Christians isolated and often opens the door for pride. You might have met people like this (or wrestled with it yourself), who have the greatest intentions—they're not evil—but their subtle complaining always taints even the greatest of truths they desire to bring. This is why deliverance and freedom from complaining will not just keep your faith alive but keep the faith of many others alive as you speak truth in love and life.

From a secular perspective, research shows that complaining could shorten your lifespan. According to a study from Harvard spanning over seven years and involving around seventy thousand women, those with a pessimistic, "glass-half-empty" outlook (aka perpetual complainers) had a higher risk of mortality on average than their optimistic, "glass-half-full" counterparts.[1]

Are you starting to see how complaining—although it can seem much smaller than all the other issues we've mentioned in previous chapters and may not seem like a big deal—really is a big deal? I've also found that complaining is often a placeholder for where praise should be. If I asked myself what the opposite of complaining was, I'd say it was praise. And praise can look like the following:

- Praise highlights the blessings in every scenario and gives God thanks.

- Praise acknowledges God and gives God thanks for every way a situation worked out, knowing that God was behind the scenes.

- Praise gives thanks for the situations God has brought you out of, and it doesn't dwell on the past.

- Praise will leave you continually filled with joy—you'll know that you were content and that you gave thanks in every situation regardless of the outcome.

- Praise is realistic through a different lens than complaining, as praise will always see the good even if the situation is not.

- Praise can express itself in outward thankfulness through your words or through just a subtle smile that shows everyone around you how grateful you are.

- Praise doesn't even have to use words; it can be shown through facial expressions and body language.

- Praise gives thanks knowing that the situation could have been worse.

- Praise always gives thanks for the reality that God works together for the good of those who love Him (Rom. 8:28).

- Praise is grateful for correction, as it will always lead you to have more of Jesus.

THE POWER OF WORDS

Out of the seventeen-plus years I have been following Jesus, I can probably count on one hand the messages I've heard preached about complaining or about the power of our words. Bill Johnson once said, "If God inhabits our praises, who inhabits our complaining?"[2] Just as praise can demolish the kingdom of darkness, complaining can be detrimental to the kingdom of God. Our words are powerful; the Scripture says that life and death are found in our tongue (Prov. 18:21). In this section of this chapter I want to speak about the importance of the words we speak to ourselves and one another.

To show you briefly how powerful our words can be, here are some verses to consider:

- "Let the *words* of my mouth and the meditation of my heart be acceptable in Your sight, O LORD, my rock and my Redeemer" (Ps. 19:14, emphasis added).

- "Keep your tongue from evil and your lips from telling lies" (Ps. 34:13, NIV).

- "Set a guard, O LORD, over my mouth; keep watch over the door of my lips" (Ps. 141:3).

And the list goes on. We know from Ephesians 4:29 that unwholesome talk should not come out of our mouths but only what is helpful for building up others according to their needs. We don't want what comes out of our mouths to cause rot or decay to ourselves or others. Before we were Christians, our tongues and words most of the time brought about death. I'm pretty sure if you recall arguments, things you might have said to others, and conversations you had before knowing Christ, you are probably very thankful they are under the blood of Jesus. Or if you think back through conversations you've had with yourself, you're probably very thankful that those words are forgiven.

A lot of times the words we speak to ourselves become realities in our lives. No, I'm not talking about new age manifestations and speaking things into existence while wearing weird crystals. I'm talking about the biblical principle of life and death being in your tongue. Words are one of the few intangible things that over time can become tangible identities in our lives. If you tell a child from when they're born that they are stupid, ugly, or good for nothing, those words will become that child's identity.

I did not grow up in a home where my self-esteem was built much by my father. I in no way intend to speak negatively, as he was not a Christian, and I do not hold him responsible for not knowing how to love me because there were many other things he did in my life that demonstrated love. But words of life were not common. As I grew older, the self-esteem I carried seemed always to be lower than everyone else's. It didn't matter how good of a musician I was; I never felt as if I was good enough. It didn't matter how in shape I was; I never felt as though it was enough.

Now that I am in my thirties and have a son, named Jedidiah, I make it my goal every day to tell him how handsome he is and how much I love him. There are times I look him in his eyes and tell him, "Do you know that you are my son and I love you so much? Do you know that I have the best son in the whole world?" I can see his mouth begin to smile and confidence fill his eyes as he says yes. My desire is that my son will grow with a confidence in God that I never carried, and that my words as his earthly father will allow him to believe and receive the words of his heavenly Father one day when I am no longer here.

As Christians our words are more powerful than we think. If you remember how God created the heavens and the earth, unlike man—whom He formed from the dust of the earth—everything you read about in Genesis 1 He created with His words. From His mouth came forth galaxies. From His mouth shot out the shining speed of light when He said, "Let there be light" (Gen. 1:3). The waters that He separated from land also came from His words. The plants, the grain, and the fruit trees all came from His words. And the Bible never says that God created seeds, which then grew. No, He literally spoke trees into existence with years and time already locked inside of them. The sun, the moon, and the stars all came from His words. The fish in the sea to the birds in the sky all came from His words. And all the other animals, large and small of every kind, came from His mouth. (See Genesis 1:1–25.)

There's a reason that the Bible speaks about the tongue the way it does. In James 3 it says, "So also the tongue is a small part of the body, and yet it boasts of great things. See how great a forest is set aflame by such a small fire! And the tongue is a fire, the very world of unrighteousness; the tongue is set among our body's parts as that which defiles the whole body and sets on fire the course of our life, and is set on fire by hell. For every species of beasts and birds, of reptiles and creatures of the sea, is tamed and has been tamed by the human race" (vv. 5–7, NASB).

Here's a quick side note that is fascinating to me, especially if you've ever been to an outdoor aquarium and you've seen the massive whales tamed by trainers. The Bible says those whales are easier to tame than our tongues. The Bible then says in verse 8, "But no one among mankind can tame the tongue; it is a restless evil, full of deadly poison" (Jas. 3, NASB).

For some, reading this verse might make things seem hopeless. As we see, the common language of today, even among the church, is complaining. But the good news in that verse we just read is that it says no human being can tame the tongue. That allows us to put our total dependence on the Lord in order to be free from complaining.

Words to Ourselves

If you grew up like me, the way you speak to yourself might be a little twisted. If you came from a home that was not very affirming with words—or worse, that put you down and destroyed you with words—you might not know how to speak to yourself because you've never been spoken to in the way God would speak to you. You might not understand that your complaining is chipping away at your very soul.

This next part I want you to read is straight from Scripture. As you read it, take it as if your heavenly Father is speaking these words over you. Let these words wash away every negative word that was spoken over you. Let them be an example of how you should see and speak over yourself from this day on. I encourage you to highlight and circle things that stand out. When you find yourself complaining, open this part of the book and read it over yourself. Also, resist the temptation to think these words are for someone else—they are indeed God's heart for you.

I recommend you find a quiet place and read this out loud to yourself.

God's Words to You

My child,

I love you! (John 3:16). I created you in my image (Genesis 1:27) and I called you "very good" (Genesis 1:31). I knit you together in your mother's womb (Psalm 139:13). I know the number of the hairs on your head (Matthew 10:30), and I am familiar with all your ways (Psalm 139:3). My precious thoughts of you are as countless as the sand on the seashore (Psalm 139:17–18).

I am Love (1 John 4:16) and the greatest commandment that I have for you is that you love (Matthew 22:37–40). My love is made complete in you when you receive my love, love me, and love others (1 John 4:7–21). To show you how to live this life of love I've given you Ten Commandments (Exodus 20:1–17), laws that honor me and are good and pleasing to you (Psalm 119)....

You see I've loved you from the beginning, long before you loved me (1 John 4:19). I sent my son Jesus, the exact representation of my being (Hebrews 1:3), to die on the cross in your place (Romans 5:8), to take upon Himself the punishment that you deserved (Isaiah 53:5), and to take away your sin (John 1:29). For you the mighty Lion sacrificed his life as an innocent Lamb (Revelation 5:5–6). Through Jesus, I, your Lord and Master, have come to serve you! (John 13:13–14)....

Indeed, I will make your righteousness shine like the dawn (Psalm 37:6). You will be a crown of glory in my hand (Isaiah 62:3), reflecting my likeness with ever-increasing glory (2 Corinthians 4:18). I am faithful to help you to be holy (1 Thessalonians 5:24) and to complete the good work I've started in you (Philippians 1:6)....

Since I care so much for you, don't worry about

getting your needs met and don't worry about tomorrow (Matthew 6:25–34). Just as I look after the little sparrow, so will I look after you (Matthew 10:26–31). So give your burdens to me and let me give you rest (Matthew 11:28). Talk to me when you're anxious and let me put you at peace (Philippians 4:6).

No matter what happens, your soul will be safe in my hands (John 10:28). Like a mother bird, I'll cover you with my feathers in my nest (Psalm 91:1–4). When rivers of difficulty roar, you will not be swept away. When fiery trials blaze, you will not be burned (Isaiah 43:2). When war breaks out, I will be your fortress, an ever-present help in trouble (Psalm 46). Even when you face death, I will take you by the hand and lead you on the joyful path to eternal life (Psalm 16:9–11).

So don't be afraid when you walk through the valley of the shadow of death, because I am your Good Shepherd. I will be with you, comforting you and protecting you on your journey (Psalm 23), and I will never leave you (Hebrews 13:5).

When enemies come against you, I will fight for you (Psalm 44:7). Even when you do what is right, people will insult you, criticize you, and mistreat you, but I will bless you (Matthew 5:11). Even when you trust your father and mother, they may forsake you, but I will receive you (Psalm 27:10). So if you find yourself poor, remember that I've blessed you with true riches (Luke 6:20). And if you find yourself last in line, remember that with me those who are last will be first! (Matthew 20:16). Yes, I will raise you up and exalt you when you are humble before me (Matthew 23:12).

When you are brokenhearted, I will draw close to you (Psalm 34:18) and cry with you (John 11:35). I'll collect all your tears in my bottle and record each one in my book (Psalm 56:8). Like a shepherd holding his lamb, I'll carry you close to my heart (Isaiah 40:11). I'll comfort you in your time of sadness (Matthew 5:4), turning your mourning into gladness (Jeremiah 31:13) and your weakness into strength (2 Corinthians 12:9-10). I will put a happy new song in your mouth (Psalm 40:3) and give you a beautiful new name (Isaiah 62:2).

Even the difficulty and pain you experience can be to your benefit if you endure these hardships as loving discipline from me, opportunities for you to be trained in the ways of righteousness and peace (Hebrews 12:6-11). Always remember that when you love me and seek my purposes, all things will work together for your good (Romans 8:28)....

With me on your side, your future is bright and full of hope! My plans are to prosper you and not to harm you (Jeremiah 29:11), to give you abundant life (John 10:10) now and forever (John 3:36). So call to me and I will answer you (Jeremiah 33:3); listen and you will hear my voice directing you (Isaiah 30:21); tune into your heart and you will sense my instructions (Psalm 16:7). My Holy Spirit will be your Counselor (John 14:15, 26; 16:7). So don't walk alone; walk in my Spirit (Galatians 5:25), trust in me, and I will direct your path (Proverbs 3:4-5) and bless you wonderfully (Ephesians 1:3)....

But you're not just my servant: you're my friend! (John 15:15) More than that, you're my beloved child! (1 John 3:1) You're precious and honored in my sight (Isaiah 43:4), and I rejoice over you with singing! (Zephaniah 3:17).

I delight in you like a bridegroom for his bride (Isaiah 62:5). I will always love you (Jeremiah 31:3) and nothing can ever change that! (Romans 8:38-39)....

Love, God.[3]

If that was the first time you've experienced such positive words spoken over your life, you might be feeling a sense of disbelief, or you might be overwhelmed with joy or tears, or just taking it all in. Regardless, I hope you experience firsthand how powerful words are. You likely noticed there wasn't one word of complaint about you in that section. There wasn't a grievance about areas you need to grow in, because you likely already know those areas. The words we speak to one another are indeed powerful.

For some, shifting away from complaining might be instantaneous, while for others it might take time, and you may often catch yourself complaining about others. Give yourself grace as the Lord leads you out of this mode of operation. As light reveals the dark areas where complaining has been hiding, you will see your life and faith in God grow immensely. You may even see your relationships shift and change as words of life begin to come out of your mouth. Take courage; we've all fallen prey to complaining, and it's something we must lay at the foot of the cross as we die daily to our flesh.

Every legend in the faith has had to die to complaining so that their words could be life-giving. We are all commanded to preach the gospel, and as the Word says, fresh water and salt water can't come from the same place (Jas. 3:11). So words of complaining and words of Christ can't come from the same place. Let grace empower you to live this out, because you will not be able to do it in your own strength. In moments of weakness He will make you strong.

Make It Personal

- What issues do you usually complain about? How can you pray about them instead?

- How might complaining be impacting your ability to experience joy and contentment?

- Reflecting on Philippians 2:14–15, how can you reframe your mindset and actions to align more closely with the call to live without grumbling or complaining?

- How can the practice of praise and gratitude serve as a countermeasure to complaining in your daily life? What are some practical steps you can take to incorporate more praise into your routine?

- Considering the power of words, how can you transform the way you speak to yourself and others to reflect more of God's love and truth?

- Have you let complaining rule your life? List every person or issue you often complain about in a journal or on a piece of paper, whether it's in your personal life, at your job, or in your family. This list may be long. Next to every complaint write a blessing for that person or issue.

Chapter 10

HOW TO DIE

THE THREE YEARS that Jesus spent with His disciples were focused on modeling to them how to lay down their lives and die to themselves. He didn't just talk about it; He demonstrated it from the beginning of His life to the end. Every miracle, and there were thirty-seven recorded in the Gospels, pointed to that.

1. Turning water into wine (John 2:1–11)
2. Healing the official's son in Capernaum (John 4:43–54)
3. Driving out the evil spirit from the man in Capernaum (Mark 1:21–27; Luke 4:34–36)
4. Healing Peter's mother-in-law (Matt. 8:14–15; Mark 1:29–31; Luke 4:38–39)
5. Healing the sick and oppressed (Matt. 8:16–17; Mark 1:32–34; Luke 4:40–41)
6. The miraculous catching of fish at the Lake of Gennesaret (Luke 5:1–11)
7. Cleansing the man with leprosy (Matt. 8:1–4; Mark 1:40–45; Luke 5:12–14)
8. Healing the centurion's paralyzed servant (Matt. 8:5–13; Luke 7:1–10)

9. Healing the paralytic man who was let down through the roof (Matt. 9:1–8; Mark 2:1–12; Luke 5:17–26)

10. Healing the man's withered hand (Matt. 12:9–14; Mark 3:1–6; Luke 6:6–11)

11. Raising the widow's dead son to life in Nain (Luke 7:11–17)

12. Calming a storm at sea (Matt. 8:23–27; Mark 4:35–41; Luke 8:22–25)

13. Casting demons into pigs (Matt. 8:28–33; Mark 5:1–20; Luke 8:26–39)

14. Healing the woman suffering from an issue of bleeding (Matt. 9:20–22; Mark 5:25–34; Luke 8:42–48)

15. Raising Jairus' daughter (Matt. 9:18, 23–26; Mark 5:21–24, 35–43; Luke 8:40–42, 49–56)

16. Healing two blind men (Matt. 9:27–31)

17. Healing a mute man (Matt. 9:32–34)

18. Healing a sick man at Bethesda (John 5:1–15)

19. Feeding the five thousand (Matt. 14:13–21; Mark 6:30–44; Luke 9:10–17; John 6:1–15)

20. Walking on water (Matt. 14:22–33; Mark 6:45–52; John 6:16–21)

21. Healing many as they touched His garment (Matt. 14:34–36; Mark 6:53–56)

22. Healing the demon-possessed daughter of a gentile woman (Matt. 15:21–28; Mark 7:24–30)

23. Healing a deaf and mute man (Mark 7:31–37)

24. Feeding the four thousand (Matt. 15:32–39; Mark 8:1–10)

25. Healing the blind man in Bethsaida (Mark 8:22–26)

26. Healing a man who was blind from birth (John 9:1–12)

27. Healing the boy possessed by an unclean spirit (Matt. 17:14–20; Mark 9:14–29; Luke 9:37–43)

28. The miracle of the temple tax money in the fish's mouth (Matt. 17:24–27)

29. Healing a mute and blind demoniac (Matt. 12:22–23; Luke 11:14–23)

30. Healing a woman crippled for eighteen years (Luke 13:10–17)

31. Healing a man on the Sabbath (Luke 14:1–6)

32. Cleansing ten lepers (Luke 17:11–19)

33. Raising Lazarus from the dead (John 11:1–45)

34. Giving Bartimaeus sight (Matt. 20:29–34; Mark 10:46–52; Luke 18:35–43)

35. The withering fig tree (Matt. 21:18–22; Mark 11:12–24)

36. Healing the servant's ear during His arrest (Luke 22:50–51)

37. The miraculous catching of fish on the Sea of Tiberias (John 21:4–11)[1]

We can see from these miracles that Jesus was never doing them to bring glory to Himself but to bring glory to the Father.

(See John 17.) Many of His miracles went against the normal cultural context, such as getting close to a man with leprosy or healing on the Sabbath. In every miracle Jesus modeled laying His life down, as each one was fueled by and rooted in sole obedience to what He saw the Father doing and heard the Father saying. It was the perfect image of a life laid down and a life that was not His own. You don't hear about Jesus waking up and asking Himself, "What am I going to do today?" I'm not saying He never had fun, but He understood the purpose of His life.

He taught His disciples that every miracle was about serving others. Jesus could have done many miracles to serve Himself, but He never did. Although I only mentioned thirty-seven miracles, there were many more. The Bible says there were so many things He did that the libraries of the world could not contain them.[2] (See John 21:25.) It might surprise you to know that the Gospels of Matthew, Mark, Luke, and John possibly account for only about fifty-two specific days of His ministry. Considering that His ministry is believed to have spanned around three years,[3] which is approximately 1,095 days, this suggests that there are many days of His activities that are not detailed in the Gospels. This aligns with John 21:25, which mentions that Jesus did many other things that were not recorded.

Every teaching that Jesus gave pointed His disciples to lay their lives down. When we think about the gospel being preached today, we sometimes picture a man on a stage giving a powerful altar call with a band. The message we would call the gospel is that Christ came, Christ died, and Christ rose again. I wouldn't disagree with that message. But do you ever wonder what Jesus preached when He preached the gospel before He had died? I've heard people say that Jesus went to the cross so we wouldn't have to, but as someone once said, He went to the cross to show you how to. I think the gospel that Jesus was preaching before He died was simply a forerunner message to

His death. He was teaching people how to lay their lives down, only to then demonstrate it on the cross.

You see, Jesus came with a message that was quite different from the Old Testament. It wasn't different because it was the opposite; it was different because He was in the process of fulfilling it. Jesus was taking the Old Testament to an entirely new level. Where the Old Testament would say, "An eye for an eye," or, "A tooth for a tooth," Jesus would say, "Turn the other cheek" (Lev. 24:19–20, paraphrased; Matt. 5:38–39, paraphrased). Where it would say, "Thou shall not murder," Jesus would say, "To hate your brother is to already have murdered him" (Matt. 5:21–22, paraphrased). There was a greater laying down of His life that Jesus demonstrated in the New Testament, which He lived as well as taught.

Some of Jesus' most famous teachings centered around the following topics:

- forgiveness (Matt. 6:14–15)
- loving your enemies (Matt. 5:44)
- the dangers of judging others (Luke 6:37–42)
- the kingdom of God (Matt. 6:33; Luke 17:20–21)
- storing our treasures in heaven (Matt. 6:19–21)
- treating others as we would want to be treated (Matt. 7:12)
- denying ourselves (Matt. 16:24)
- loving others (Matt. 22:39)
- not loving money, as it's the root of all evil (Matt. 6:24; 1 Tim. 6:10)
- servanthood (Matt. 23:11–12)

- Gaining God is more important than gaining the world (Matt. 16:26).

- Religion doesn't save or make a man holy, as the external has little to do with what happens on the inside of a man or woman (Matt. 15:11-13; 23:25-26).

- teaching us on the greatest commandments, which are to love God above everything and love others as yourself (Matt. 22:37-39; Mark 12:28-31)

Do you see how these teachings have very little to do with creating comfort for the disciples? They had little to do with creating an environment in which the disciples would have little resistance. Jesus must have known something that they didn't. He must have understood the fulfillment of laying down your life and how when you do that, then and only then will you find your life. It almost seemed as if Jesus made it difficult to follow Him. If we remember the story of the rich young ruler, Jesus said he must go sell everything (Matt. 19:16-22). He knew that tricking people into following Him wouldn't make disciples—it would make disasters.

We can see that through His parables, Jesus was leading us to lay our lives down and teaching us how to die to ourselves. He did this by bringing culturally relevant stories that the Jews would have understood but also that we can relate to two thousand years later.

Let's look at Jesus' parables:

- He gave the parable of the new cloth and wineskin in Matthew 9:16-17, breaking the lie that His message would come and build upon their traditions and practices.

- He gave the parable of the lampstand in Mark 4:21–22, implying that we shouldn't waste our light and the oil it would take to light that lamp. Our light should clearly shine to the world, proclaiming our faith.

- He gave the parable of the wise and foolish builders in Luke 6:47–49, emphasizing the importance of building our homes on solid foundations and promising storms would come.

- He gave the parable of the sower in Mark 4:3–20, breaking down the types of hearts that we would encounter.

- He gave the parable of the weeds in Matthew 13:24–30 and 36–43, warning us not to judge people and that He will be the One to sort everything out in the end.

- He gave the parable of the mustard seed in Luke 13:18–19, explaining that the kingdom of God, although starting small in the hearts of people, could change the entire world.

- He gave the parable of the leaven in Luke 13:20–21, illustrating how the kingdom of God would start small and grow immensely.

- He gave the parable of the hidden treasure and the pearl in Matthew 13:44–46, explaining the value of God's kingdom and our willingness to give up everything to find it.

- He gave the parable of the net in Matthew 13:47–50, showing how we would be fishers of men and see souls saved; He shows how in the end, the real disciples will be separated from the false.

- He gave the parable of the homeowner in Matthew 13:52, illustrating the connection between the teachings of the Old Testament prophecies and Christ's new covenant.

- He gave the parable of the wandering sheep in Matthew 18:12-14, reiterating His care for even the ones who stray.

- He gave the parable of the unmerciful servant in Matthew 18:23-35, warning us to forgive.

- He gave the parable of the workers in the vineyard in Matthew 20:1-16, showing that He is the One who compensates us for our work and that we should not focus on our brothers and sisters around us.

- He gave the parable of the two sons in Matthew 21:28-31, showing how the outward expression of compliance means nothing compared with inward repentance.

- He gave the parable of the vineyard tenants in Mark 12:1-11, emphasizing the importance of stewarding the people of God and His servants.

- He gave the parable of the wedding banquet in Matthew 22:1-14, illustrating how He opens up the invitation to the gentiles to receive the kingdom of God.

- He gave the parable of the fig tree in Mark 13:28-33, using it to show us the signs that the end is coming.

- He gave the parable of the ten virgins in Matthew 25:1–13, teaching about being prepared for His coming.

- He gave the parable of the talents in Luke 19:12–27, teaching us to be responsible for stewarding what is given to us.

- He gave the parable of the sheep and goats in Matthew 25:31–46, teaching how people will be separated at the end of the age.

- He gave the parable of the growing seed in Mark 4:26–29, illustrating how the kingdom of heaven will grow amid the world's kingdom.

- He gave the parable of the returning homeowner in Mark 13:34–37, teaching us to be watchful for the return of our Master.

- He gave the parable of the moneylender in Luke 7:41–43, addressing love and how debts are forgiven—those who are forgiven much love much.

- He gave the parable of the rich fool in Luke 12:16–21, showing how the rich don't always make the best decisions in light of eternity.

- He gave the parable of the watchful servants in Luke 12:35–40, teaching us to be watchful for the second coming.

- He gave the parable of the wise and foolish servants in Luke 12:42–48, addressing His disciples and urging them to be about their Master's business when He returns.

- He gave the parable of the master and his servant in Luke 17:7-10, showing how God owes us nothing but we owe everything to God.

- He gave the parable of the good Samaritan in Luke 10:30-37, shocking the disciples with who actually stops to help.

- He gave the parable of the friend seeking bread in Luke 11:5-8, teaching His disciples to make bold requests and to pray until God moves.

- He gave the parable of the place of honor in Luke 14:7-1, teaching us not to put ourselves in places of honor but to take the low place and then be asked to move up.

- He gave the parable of the great banquet in Luke 14:16-24, showing how if we miss the invitation, someone else will take that place.

- He gave the parable of counting the cost in Luke 14:28-33, urging us to count the cost of following Him, lest we are unable to complete it.

- He gave the parable of the lost coin in Luke 15:8-10, showing the importance of searching for the one who is lost.

- He gave the parable of the shrewd manager in Luke 16:1-9, illustrating that we are not to lay up treasures on earth but in heaven.

- He gave the parable of the prodigal son in Luke 15:11-32, showing how the father celebrates his return, while the other son doesn't realize his identity and what he's had all along.

- He gave the parable of the rich man and Lazarus in Luke 16:19–31, teaching that wealth isn't everything in life.

- He gave the parable of the persistent widow in Luke 18:2–8, teaching how the judge grants her request because she is persistent.

- Lastly, He gave the parable of the Pharisee and the tax collector in Luke 18:10–14, showing how when two men go up to pray, God hears the humble one.

Whether it was His miracles, His teachings, or His parables, Jesus was constantly pointing us to lay our lives down and die to ourselves. Now, I know that Jesus had His heavenly Father to look to for what He would do and say. But there was also someone in Jesus' life that we overlook, who was probably one of the greatest tangible, physical examples of Jesus in laying down his life. This individual was not given much credit, and we don't really hear much about his life. His name is Joseph, and he was Jesus' stepdad.

A descendant of David, Joseph was a carpenter in Nazareth and did not have the most ideal marriage engagement. (See Matthew 1:18–20 and 13:55.) After finding out the woman he was about to marry was pregnant, I'm pretty sure he wasn't too excited right away. He might have even questioned her honesty in her claim regarding the divine nature of her child's conception. Still, through it all you don't see Joseph lose his cool or get angry. Even as he planned to serve Mary a certificate of divorce, the Bible says he was going to do it with honor in secret (Matt. 1:19).

After coming to grips with the fact that the Holy Spirit really did impregnate his wife-to-be (only after being visited by an angel, because let's be honest, that's probably the only thing that would make a man believe that story), Joseph demonstrated himself as a nurturer and protector who didn't let the testimony of his wife get tainted (Matt. 1:20–25). He then went through nine months of pregnancy with Mary, probably having many questions filling his mind. Would his *yes* remain the same?

The distress and anxiety he might have felt were real, and then, to top it off, the only place he could find for the child to be born was a manger, as there was no room at the inn (Luke 2:7). After enduring all that, he found himself fleeing to protect the life of his Son, who wasn't even biologically his (Matt. 2:13–15). Imagine the responsibility he felt—it's one thing to bear the weight of caring for your own son, but imagine having the responsibility of laying your life down and raising the Son of God.

Some believe that "according to the tradition of the Orthodox Church, Joseph died before Jesus began [His] ministry."[4] Imagine raising this boy for over twenty years, laying your life down for Him, fathering Him, and then never getting to see the full potential of what that boy would become. Talk about a life laid down. Talk about dying daily. This is a man who did not live his life for himself. He took up the very assignment of God and fulfilled it. He was a great example to Jesus of an earthly father.

Ways to Die Daily

You might have grown up seeing sacrificial love and witnessing people who modeled the Bible's teachings. Or you might not have had examples of people teaching you how to die daily or showing you sacrificial love. You might not have seen this in the churches you attended or from leaders on social media. I wanted to give you the most practical examples of what we are to die to daily.

Here is a list of things to help you know what to crucify on a daily basis. The Bible says to crucify our flesh daily, but often we need reminding of what *flesh* means (Luke 9:23; Gal. 5:24). As we've discussed throughout this book, dying to our flesh is not talking about our skin; it refers to the works of the flesh, as mentioned in Galatians 5:19–21. These are things that will kill your faith. Here are the desires of the flesh that we are to die to daily and keep at the forefront of our minds as we run the good race of our faith.

We are to die to the following:

- **Sexual immorality.** The Greek word is *porneia*, which includes adultery, fornication, and homosexuality.[5]

- **Impurity.** The Greek word is *akatharsia*, which includes lust for things that are impure, such as luxurious and profligate living, and having impure motives.[6]

- **Sensuality.** The Greek word is *aselgeia*, which means "shameless" sinning.[7]

- **Idolatry.** The Greek word is *eidōlolatria*, which means "the worship of false gods" and also the worshipping of mammon,[8] which refers to wealth and riches.

- **Sorcery.** The Greek word is *pharmakeia*, which refers to drug use or "magical arts."[9]

- **Enmity.** The Greek word is *echthra*, which means hostility and hatred.[10]

- **Strife.** The Greek word is *eris*, which means debate or quarreling.[11]

- **Jealousy.** The Greek word is *zēlos*, which means "fierceness of indignation."[12]

- **Bursts of anger.** The Greek word is *thymos*, which means "anger...boiling up."[13]
- **Rivalries.** The Greek word is *eritheia*, which means disputes and divisive, "selfish ambition."[14]
- **Dissension.** The Greek word is *dichostasia*, which means disunion and division.[15]
- **Divisions.** The Greek word is *hairesis*, which means heresy.[16]
- **Envy.** The Greek word is *phthonos*, which means spite.[17]
- **Drunkenness.** The Greek word is *methē*, which means intoxication.[18]
- **Orgies.** The Greek word is *kōmos*, which means reveling or rioting (aka letting loose).[19]

These works of the flesh are found to varying degrees in each of us as part of our human nature. We must remember, as Romans 5:10 says, "For if while we were enemies we were reconciled to God by the death of his Son, much more, now that we are reconciled, shall we be saved by his life" (ESV). Can you see how the works of our flesh are by-products of us being enemies of God? When Jesus died, He made a way for us to be not His enemies but His friends. He made a way for us to become His sons and daughters. The works of the flesh are not a burdensome thing to die to; it's a joy to lay down at the cross of Calvary that which was never ours to bear.

A Disclaimer for the Struggling

Do not be discouraged if you are struggling in any of these areas; rather, rejoice that the Holy Spirit is illuminating them to you and that you are working to overcome. I have come to find that struggling with your sin often is one of the greatest indications that you are a true believer and that the Holy Spirit dwells in you. If the Holy Spirit did not dwell in you and there was no struggle, you would just willfully give in to that sin. The Holy Spirit is what enables you to put up a fight with your flesh, ultimately crucifying it to the cross. Struggling with sin as a believer is far different from giving in to it and willfully accepting it as your lifestyle.

I once heard an analogy: If you were to crucify yourself daily, you would know that a cross requires three nails. I'm speaking metaphorically, although the cross was literal. If you were able to hammer the nail in your feet and then one in your left hand, you would still have your right hand open, which means you would require someone else to help crucify you. Sometimes the things you are going through require a friend to come and help nail your works of the flesh to the cross. That might look like them praying with you, fasting with you, reading the Word with you, and helping you see the truth when you can't see it for yourself. Godly friends and family are often placed by God in our lives to help make sure that the old versions of us stay dead and are never resurrected.

How to Stay Dead

There are many things within our Christianity, our lives, and our culture that will try to resurrect our old man and bring back to today what the cross has slain. There are many situations that will try to bring back your old mindsets, your old way of thinking, your old nature, your old conversations, and your old relationships. The things that you left at the cross will sometimes come right back, knocking at your door. Many things will try to wash away the blood that washed us white as snow, and there will be many moments that tempt us to go back to who we were. I want to share another story with you, from my friend Todd White. He carries a powerful testimony about dying to his flesh.

TODD WHITE

The reality of the Christian life is summed up in one word, and that is *death*. And death is something that a lot of people are afraid of, but the truth is that death at the end of a Christian life is only the beginning. But death at the beginning of a Christian life is the true beginning of an authentic relationship with Jesus. The only way that you can do this is by surrendering your everything to Him. That means dying to self.

Self is one of the biggest issues on the planet. And one of the major reasons that people can't live their lives out loud for God is the reality of self-consciousness—just the reality of the self-serving attitude. The truth is, when you come to Him, you have to understand that you've been cultivating the wisdom of man your whole life—you've learned the way that seems right to a man. That way leads to destruction. So when somebody gets born again, they come into a brand-new way of living that comes through a brand-new way of thinking.

"The flesh profits nothing"—that's what Jesus said (John 6:63, NKJV). It's all about the Spirit of God. So when He refers to the flesh, He's referring to the way that seems right to a man, or the carnal mind of a man. You have a war that you're in, and the only way to win this war is to wage war in the spirit. The truth of what God says is the reality of where we need to live from. The wisdom of man and the wisdom of God are two totally different things. James 3:15–16 (NKJV) says the wisdom of man is "sensual" and "demonic"; it's full of "self-seeking" and "envy," and "every evil thing [is] there." It doesn't say "some"; it says "every evil thing."

Aren't we supposed to war against evil? Aren't we supposed to stand up for what is right and make sure that we tear down what's evil?

The Christian life is all about learning what the wisdom of God is. It's "peaceable, gentle, willing to yield, full of...good fruits, without partiality and without hypocrisy" (Jas. 3:17, NKJV). Hypocrisy is something that everybody has to deal with. The truth is that you can't incorporate Jesus into your life; you must surrender everything. Any place that you hold on to in your life is a target for the enemy. You will be a fifty-fifty Christian—fifty in and fifty out. Then your fifty out becomes fifty-five out, and you're forty-five in; then it moves to sixty and forty, and then it moves to thirty-five. All of a sudden, your life is full of compromise.

You have to find out what the truth is that God says—not to be "conformed to this world" but to be "transformed by the renewing of your mind" (Rom. 12:2, NKJV). That's Romans 12:2. But don't forget it comes after Romans 12:1, and Romans 12:1 says, "Offer your bodies as a living sacrifice, holy and [acceptable]," which is your reasonable and pleasing service to God (NIV). The only reasonable service we have is to offer our bodies as a living sacrifice. Now, as a sacrifice, we have to willingly get up on the altar from our own free will and lay our lives down.

It's a beautiful picture of what Jesus did: He laid His life down. No one took it from him. God's asking us to do what His Son did. "God so loved the world that he gave his one and only Son, that whoever believes in him shall not perish but have eternal life" (John 3:16, NIV). Eternal life begins with meeting the Father; when you meet the Father, you can no longer live for yourself, but you live for the One that gave Himself.

Galatians 2:20 states, "I have been crucified with

Christ and I no longer live," but the life that I do live, "I live by faith in the Son of God, who…gave himself for me" (NIV). That would be Jesus. We need to live the crucified life—crucified to our own ambitions and crucified to our own ideas. We need to surrender and submit everything to the Lord so that we can absolutely deny ourselves. Paul says that "to live is Christ and to die is gain" in Philippians 1:21. He describes this life that is absolutely necessary. "To live is Christ and to die is gain." If "to die is gain," why wouldn't we all want to do it?

What needs to go is the way that seems right to man. Be renewed in the spirit of your mind, and don't be conformed to the world, but be transformed and make sure that you can start to think like God. Set your mind on things above and not on those beneath. This Christian life can only be lived one way—it's the cross. The cross is the reality of every Christian's life. Jesus says that we are supposed to pick up our crosses and follow Him, but the only way we can do that is by denying ourselves (Matt. 16:24). And denying ourselves means denying the ways that we've been raised, the cultures we grew up in, and all the things that you thought were right.

Looking at the gospel through the picture of Jesus' life, you see what's really right. There's a way that seems right to a man, but the way that is right to God is righteousness. When you step in and see that you've been made right with God, there is nothing in this world that becomes tasteful because you've finally tasted and seen that the Lord is good. You can surrender everything. You can give your heart to Jesus, and you can give your life to Jesus. Right now is the time you can actually say, "Lord Jesus, I do not want to live the life I've been living, but I want to live the authentic Christian life. Help me live a crucified life where I die to myself so that I can live unto You. Help me realize what it means to live as Christ and to die in order to gain." One day when I put off this tent, I'm going to stand before Him and He's going to say, "Well done," and that's what every Christian brother and sister needs to hear on that day.

Legends Die Young

As this book comes to a close, I hope you've journeyed through the Scriptures and had many conversations with the Holy Spirit about the topics we've discussed. I hope you wrestled with the challenging subjects and now find joy and excitement in laying your life down for Christ. I hope your priorities have shifted and you feel a stronger inclination to obey God.

As I mentioned in the introduction, the title of this book, *Legends Die Young*, is inspired by the legends of the faith who are legendary because they dared to lay their lives down daily for Jesus. I have pondered, "What is a legend? Who are legends to me?" Whether they are black, white, Hispanic, Christians in the political realm or in ministry, or even a mom or dad I know, they all share a common thread: They laid down their lives.

We often glamorize legends for their cars, homes, or wealth, or the impact they've made in the world. We highlight their successes without recognizing that those monumental moments were built on countless small, faithful acts of giving a little more every single day.

As Christians it is our honor to follow in the footsteps of the greatest legend: Jesus Christ. He walked the earth, died on the cross, and rose again. He was a legend who died young, at the age of thirty-three, but He also died young much earlier in His life. From His earliest account at age twelve in the temple to His last moments on the cross, we see a man who was continually about His Father's business. His greatest desire was to bring His Father joy. May our lives mirror His, bringing joy to the Father. May He find faith when He comes to the earth, and may the Lamb receive the reward of His suffering.

Make It Personal

- What does it mean to truly die to self in your everyday life?

- What areas of your life is God calling you to lay down in obedience to Him? What is keeping you from surrendering those parts of your life? How might the enemy gain a grip on your life because you refuse to die to self in those areas?

- How do the miracles of Jesus demonstrate the principle of laying down one's life and dying to self? How can you apply this principle to your daily life?

- What practical steps can you take to daily crucify the works of the flesh in your own life?

- How can we, like Joseph, remain faithful and obedient to God, even when we do not fully understand His plans or see immediate results?

- How does the struggle against the works of the flesh reveal your need to rely on the Holy Spirit? How can you actively seek His guidance in overcoming your weaknesses?

NOTES

Introduction
1. Michael Miller, in communication with the author.

Chapter 1
1. *Merriam-Webster*, s.v. "deconstruction," accessed July 1, 2024, https://www.merriam-webster.com/dictionary/deconstruction.
2. Subby Szterszky, "Deconstruction: A Look at a Popular and Polarizing Concept," Focus on the Family Canada, accessed June 28, 2024, https://www.focusonthefamily.ca/content/deconstruction-a-look-at-a-popular-and-polarizing-concept.
3. *Merriam-Webster*, s.v. "deconstruction."

Chapter 2
1. Bible Hub, s.v. "605. apokatastasis," accessed July 3, 2024, https://biblehub.com/greek/605.htm.
2. "Thirty Pieces of Silver," Wikipedia, modified June 21, 2024, https://en.wikipedia.org/wiki/Thirty_pieces_of_silver.
3. Mary Stevenson, "Footprints in the Sand," Footprints in the Sand, Audrey Ostoyic, accessed July 2, 2024, https://footprintssandpoem.com/mary-stevenson-version-of-footprints-in-the-sand/.
4. Stevenson, "Footprints in the Sand."
5. Blue Letter Bible, s.v. "*syschēmatizō*," accessed July 2, 2024, https://www.blueletterbible.org/lexicon/g4964/kjv/tr/0-1/.
6. Bible Hub, s.v. "342. anakainósis," accessed July 2, 2024, https://biblehub.com/greek/342.htm.
7. Iain De Jong, "Eligibility Does NOT Equal Entitlement," OrgCode, accessed July 3, 2024, https://www.orgcode.com/blog/eligibility-does-not-equal-entitlement#:~:text=Eligibility%20means%20the%20state%20of,(again%20my%20emphasis%20added).

8. Blue Letter Bible, s.v. "*airō*," accessed July 3, 2024, https://www.blueletterbible.org/lexicon/g142/kjv/tr/0-1/.
9. Donavyn Coffey, "Why Does Christianity Have So Many Denominations?" Live Science, accessed July 3, 2024, https://www.livescience.com/christianity-denominations.html.
10. Bryce Anderson—Topic, "The Word Within the Word (feat. Loren Cunningham)," YouTube, October 11, 2016, https://www.youtube.com/watch?app=desktop&v=2o-73jSzFjg.
11. Bill Mounce, s.v. "μετανοέω," accessed July 3, 2024, https://www.billmounce.com/greek-dictionary/metanoeo.

Chapter 3

1. Bible Hub, s.v. "1818. exapataó," accessed July 3, 2024, https://biblehub.com/greek/1818.htm.
2. Jesus Image (@jesus_image) and Jesus Image Church (@jesusimagechurch), "We are so grateful for the Lord and His faithfulness!" Instagram video, August 15, 2022, https://www.instagram.com/p/ChTQzSGsubM/?igsh=MTNvMzRtY3F2bmVrNA==.
3. Jesus Image (@jesus_image) and Jesus Image Church (@jesusimagechurch), "We are so grateful for the Lord and His faithfulness!"
4. Jesus Image (@jesus_image) and Jesus Image Church (@jesusimagechurch), "We are so grateful for the Lord and His faithfulness!"
5. Elvina Hall, "Jesus Paid It All," Hymnary.org, accessed July 17, 2024, https://hymnary.org/text/i_hear_the_savior_say_thy_strength_indee.

Chapter 4

1. King James Bible Dictionary, s.v. "salvation," accessed July 9, 2024, https://kingjamesbibledictionary.com/Dictionary/salvation; King James Bible Dictionary, s.v. "hope," accessed July 9, 2024, https://kingjamesbibledictionary.com/Dictionary/hope; King James Bible Dictionary, s.v. "faith," accessed

July 9, 2024, https://kingjamesbibledictionary.com/Dictionary/faith; King James Bible Dictionary, s.v. "trust," accessed July 9, 2024, https://kingjamesbibledictionary.com/Dictionary/trust.
2. John Bechtle, "Paradidomi: Hand It Over!," Ezra Project, accessed July 9, 2024, https://ezraproject.com/paradidomi-hand-it-over/#:~:text=In%20Greek%2C%20the%20word%20commonly,to%20deliver%20or%20pass%20down.
3. Blue Letter Bible, s.v. "pešaʿ," accessed July 9, 2024, https://www.blueletterbible.org/lexicon/h6588/kjv/wlc/0-1/.
4. The Bible Project, "Transgression," YouTube, May 10, 2018, https://www.youtube.com/watch?v=cq-r9FFN5ew.
5. The Bible Project, "Transgression."
6. For various instances of betrayal in the Bible, see Genesis 3, Genesis 4:1–16, Genesis 37, 1 Samuel 19–24, and Matthew 26:14–16, 47–50.

Chapter 5

1. Vitor Belfort, "Vitor Belfort Quotes," BrainyQuote, accessed July 10, 2024, https://www.brainyquote.com/quotes/vitor_belfort_978008.
2. Blue Letter Bible, s.v. "hystereō," accessed July 10, 2024, https://www.blueletterbible.org/lexicon/g5302/kjv/tr/0-1/.
3. Blue Letter Bible, s.v. "miainō," accessed July 10, 2024, https://www.blueletterbible.org/lexicon/g3392/kjv/tr/0-1/.
4. "Bitterness (4088) pikría," SermonIndex.net, accessed July 10, 2024, https://www.sermonindex.net/modules/articles/index.php?view=article&aid=33617.
5. "Bitterness (4088) pikría," SermonIndex.net.
6. Herbert Lockyer, *All the Promises of the Bible* (Grand Rapids, MI: Zondervan Publishing House, 1975), 10.

Chapter 6

1. Jud Davis, "God 10,000 Talents and Forgiving a Sinning Brother," *The Herald-News*, November 3, 2015, https://www.rheaheraldnews.com/lifestyles/article_334f283e-8262-11e5-aaf7-53cf9a2b76bb.html.
2. Blue Letter Bible, s.v. "*paraptōma*," accessed July 17, 2024, https://www.blueletterbible.org/lexicon/g3900/kjv/tr/0-1/.
3. J. Harold Greenlee, "'More Than These?' John 21:15," Journal of Translation 1, no. 2 (2005): 19–20, https://www.sil.org/system/files/reapdata/17/00/45/170045653181104208428365 6306957500 61511/siljot2005_2_02.pdf.
4. "John 21:15: What Does John 21:15 Mean?," BibleRef, accessed July 11, 2024, https://www.bibleref.com/John/21/John-21-15.html.
5. R. T. Kendall, *Total Forgiveness* (Lake Mary, FL: Charisma House, 2007), 163–171.
6. R. T. Kendall, *Total Forgiveness*, 3–18.

Chapter 7

1. Mary Fairchild, "Timeline of Jesus' Death," Learn Religions, last modified February 4, 2020, https://www.learnreligions.com/timeline-of-jesus-death-700226; Kyle Richter, "What Happened on Good Friday? A Timeline of Jesus's Last Day," The Crossing Church, April 7, 2022, https://info.thecrossingchurch.com/blog/what-happened-on-good-friday-a-timeline-of-jesuss-crucifixion.
2. *The Passion of the Christ*, directed by Mel Gibson (Rome: Icon Productions, 2004), https://www.amazon.com/gp/video/detail/amzn1.dv.gti.5ea9f676-fc0a-b350-2a33-76f86ce5e3ea?autoplay=0&ref_=atv_cf_strg_wb.
3. Christian Pure Team, "The Fates of the Disciples: How Each of Jesus' Apostles Met Their End," Christian Pure, accessed July 12, 2024, https://www.christianpure.com/learn/disciples-fates-jesus-apostles-deaths.

4. Christian Pure Team, "The Fates of the Disciples."
5. Andrew Jackson, "Apostle Philip," Dr. Andrew Jackson, accessed July 12, 2024, https://www.drandrewjackson.com/the-apostle-philip-and-his-martydom/; "The Apostle Philip Martyred at Hierapolis," Today's Catholic, September 20, 2011, https://todayscatholic.org/the-apostle-philip-martyred-at-hierapolis/. According to the *Acts of Philip* (as referenced in "Apostle Philip"), Philip was arrested by the Roman authorities and cruelly tortured. Tradition holds that he was crucified upside down around the year AD 80 in Hierapolis, Greece. This account is supported by various sources, including Today's Catholic and Dr. Andrew Jackson.
6. "Death of the Apostles," Bible.org, accessed July 12, 2024, https://bible.org/illustration/death-apostles. According to this source, "Matthew suffered martyrdom by being slain with a sword at a distant city of Ethiopia." The source provides accounts of the deaths of various apostles, including Matthew.
7. Christian Pure Team, "The Fates of the Disciples"; Edward Smither, "How Suffering Led Armenians to Christ," Desiring God, May 20, 2023, https://www.desiringgod.org/articles/how-suffering-led-armenians-to-christ.
8. Christian Pure Team, "The Fates of the Disciples."
9. Ryan Nelson, "Who Was Simon the Zealot? The Beginner's Guide," Overview Bible, August 7, 2019, https://overviewbible.com/simon-the-zealot/; Christian Pure Team, "The Fates of the Disciples."
10. Ryan Nelson, "Who Was Matthias the Apostle? The Beginner's Guide," Overview Bible, September 10, 2019, https://overviewbible.com/matthias-the-apostle/.
11. Christian Pure Team, "The Fates of the Disciples"; Acts 12:1–2; Matthew 17:1–2.
12. Jeremy Walker, "Suffering with Christ," Table Talk, accessed July 13, 2024, https://tabletalkmagazine.com/article/2020/10/suffering-with-christ/.

13. Bible Hub, s.v. "3404. miseó," accessed July 14, https://biblehub.com/greek/3404.htm.
14. Blue Letter Bible, s.v. "*aphorizō*," accessed July 14, 2024, https://www.blueletterbible.org/lexicon/g873/kjv/tr/0-1/.
15. Blue Letter Bible, s.v. "*oneidizō*," accessed July 14, 2024, https://www.blueletterbible.org/lexicon/g3679/kjv/tr/0-1/.
16. Bible Hub, s.v. "1544. ekballo," accessed July 14, 2024, https://biblehub.com/greek/1544.htm.
17. John Bechtle, "Martus—A Call to Martyrdom?," Ezra Project, December 26, 2020, https://ezraproject.com/martus-a-call-to-martyrdom/; Bible Hub, s.v. "3144. martus," accessed July 14, 2024, https://biblehub.com/greek/3144.htm.
18. DC Talk and Voice of the Martyrs, *Jesus Freaks: Stories of Those Who Stood for Jesus, the Ultimate Jesus Freaks* (Ada, MI: Bethany House Publishers, 2020).
19. DC Talk and Voice of the Martyrs, *Jesus Freaks*, 177–178; "Laurence Saunders," Prabook, accessed July 18, 2024, https://prabook.com/web/laurence.saunders/2150873; "Stories of Christian Martyrs: John Brown," The Voice of the Martyrs, September 27, 2022, https://www.persecution.com/stories/stories-of-christian-martyrs-john-brown/; "Lying to an Enemy," Teleios Ministries, accessed July 14, 2024, https://www.teleiosministries.com/pdfs/Misc/lie_to_enemy.pdf; "Stories of Christian Martyrs: Redoy Roy," The Voice of the Martyrs, August 24, 2021, https://www.persecution.com/stories/stories-of-christian-martyrs-redoy-roy/; "Indonesia: Reverend Wau (9 June 2003)," Voice of the Martyrs, June 9, 2024, https://vom.com.au/stories/indonesia-reverend-wau/; Justus Reid Weiner, *Human Rights of Christians in Palestinian Society* (Jerusalem: Jerusalem Center for Public Affairs and Yuval Press, 2005), v; "China: Jiang Zongxiu (17 June 2004)," Voice of the Martyrs, June 18, 2023, https://vom.com.au/stories/china-jiang-zongxiu/#:~:text=Jiang%20Zongxiu%2C%20a%2034-year-old%20woman%2C%20was%20arrested%20for,officers%20at%20their%20office%20in%20the%20neighbouring%20province; "Christian Store

Manager Martyred in Gaza City," The Voice of the Martyrs, October 8, 2007, https://www.persecutionblog.com/2007/10/christian-store.html; "Colombia: Manuel Camacho," Voice of the Martyrs, September 21, 2023, https://vom.com.au/stories/remembering-martyrs-manuel-camacho-colombia/; "Stories of Christian Martyrs: Rocio Pino," The Voice of the Martyrs, August 24, 2021, https://www.persecution.com/stories/stories-of-christian-martyrs-rocio-pino/; "Mathayo Kachili," Voice of the Martyrs, February 20, 2024, https://vom.com.au/stories/mathayo-kachili-february-2013/; Staff writer, "Christian Leaders Remember 21 Men Martyred by ISIS in Libya," Christian Today, accessed July 14, 2024, https://www.christiantoday.com/article/christian.leaders.remember.21.men.martyred.by.isis.in.libya/136387.htm; "Stories of Christian Martyrs: Pastor Gideon Periyaswamy," The Voice of the Martyrs, March 16, 2022, https://www.persecution.com/stories/stories-of-christian-martyrs-pastor-gideon-periyaswamy/; "Stories of Christian Martyrs: Surabaya Church Bombings," The Voice of the Martyrs, April 27, 2022, https://www.persecution.com/stories/stories-of-christian-martyrs-surabaya-church-bombings/.

CHAPTER 9

1. Eric Kim et al., "Optimism and Cause-Specific Mortality: A Prospective Cohort Study," *American Journal of Epidemiology* 185, no. 1 (January 2017): 21–29, https://doi.org/10.1093/aje/kww182.
2. Bill Johnson, "If God inhabits our praises, who inhabits our complaining?" Facebook photo, September 20, 2019, https://www.facebook.com/BillJohnsonMinistries/photos/a.432919458386/10157093387233387/?type=3.
3. Bill Gaultiere, "God's Love Letter to You!" Soul Shepherding, accessed July 15, 2024, https://www.soulshepherding.org/gods-love-letter-to-you/.

Chapter 10

1. Mary Fairchild, "Miracles of Jesus: From Healing the Sick to Turning Water Into Wine," Learn Religions, modified December 5, 2022, https://www.learnreligions.com/miracles-of-jesus-700158.
2. John 21:25, NIV; John Barnett, "Seven Days from the Life of Christ," SermonSearch, accessed July 16, 2024, https://www.sermonsearch.com/sermon-outlines/64511/seven-days-from-the-life-of-christ/. According to the Gospel of John, "Jesus did many other things as well. If every one of them were written down, I suppose that even the whole world would not have room for the books that would be written" (21:25, NIV). It is estimated by scholars like John Barnett that the Gospels only account for a small fraction of the days Jesus spent in ministry, which would leave many unrecorded days that were likely spent teaching and guiding His disciples.
3. John Barnett, "Seven Days from the Life of Christ"; "What Was the Length of Jesus' Public Ministry?" Compelling Truth, accessed July 16, 2024, https://www.compellingtruth.org/length-Jesus-ministry.html; "How Long was Jesus' Ministry?" Got Questions, accessed July 16, 2024, https://www.gotquestions.org/length-Jesus-ministry.html.
4. "What Happened to Joseph, Jesus' Father?," StackExchange: Christianity, accessed July 16, 2024, https://christianity.stackexchange.com/questions/33283/what-happened-to-joseph-jesus-father; "Joseph the Betrothed," Orthodox Wiki, accessed July 16, 2024, https://orthodoxwiki.org/Joseph_the_Betrothed. Semi-anonymous writers from StackExchange: Christianity state, "According to the tradition of the Orthodox Church, Joseph died before Jesus began [His] ministry." Orthodox Wiki offers support for this statement.
5. Blue Letter Bible, s.v. "*porneia*," accessed July 16, 2024, https://www.blueletterbible.org/lexicon/g4202/kjv/tr/0-1/.

6. Blue Letter bible, s.v. "*akatharsia*," accessed July 16, 2024, https://www.blueletterbible.org/lexicon/g167/kjv/tr/0-1/.
7. "Galatians 5:19: NASB Lexicon," Bible Hub, accessed July 16, 2024, https://biblehub.com/lexicon/galatians/5-19.htm; "What Does Galatians 5:19 Mean?" BibleRef, accessed July 16, 2024, https://www.bibleref.com/Galatians/5/Galatians-5-19.html.
8. Blue Letter Bible, s.v. "*eidōlolatria*," accessed July 16, 2024, https://www.blueletterbible.org/lexicon/g1495/kjv/tr/0-1/.
9. Blue Letter Bible, s.v. "*pharmakeia*," accessed July 16, 2024, https://www.blueletterbible.org/lexicon/g5331/kjv/tr/0-1/.
10. Blue Letter Bible, s.v. "*echthra*," accessed July 16, 2024, https://www.blueletterbible.org/lexicon/g2189/kjv/tr/0-1/.
11. Blue Letter Bible, s.v. "*eris*," accessed July 16, 2024, https://www.blueletterbible.org/lexicon/g2054/kjv/tr/0-1/.
12. Blue Letter Bible, s.v. "*zēlos*," accessed July 16, 2024, https://www.blueletterbible.org/lexicon/g2205/kjv/tr/0-1/.
13. "Galatians 5:20: NASB Lexicon," Bible Hub, accessed July 16, 2024, https://biblehub.com/lexicon/galatians/5-20.htm; Blue Letter Bible, s.v. "*thymos*," accessed July 16, 2024, https://www.blueletterbible.org/lexicon/g2372/kjv/tr/0-1/.
14. Bible Hub, s.v. "2052. eritheia," accessed July 17, 2024, https://biblehub.com/greek/2052.htm.
15. Blue Letter Bible, s.v. "*dichostasia*," accessed July 16, 2024, https://www.blueletterbible.org/lexicon/g1370/kjv/tr/0-1/.
16. Bill Mounce, s.v. "αἵρεσις," accessed July 16, 2024, https://www.billmounce.com/greek-dictionary/hairesis.
17. Blue Letter Bible, s.v. "*phthonos*," accessed July 16, 2024, https://www.blueletterbible.org/lexicon/g5355/kjv/tr/0-1/.
18. Blue Letter Bible, s.v. "*methē*," accessed July 16, 2024, https://www.blueletterbible.org/lexicon/g3178/kjv/tr/0-1/.
19. Bill Mounce, s.v. "κῶμος," accessed July 16, 2024, https://www.billmounce.com/greek-dictionary/komos; Blue Letter Bible, s.v. "*kōmos*," accessed July 16, 2024, https://www.blueletterbible.org/lexicon/g2970/kjv/tr/0-1/.